To Free This Mind...

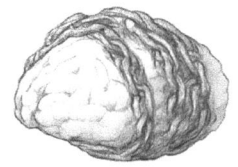

(A Dialogue — Dr. Muhammad Shahzad and Dr. Baland Iqbal)

Copyright © 2023 by Dr. Baland Iqbal

All rights reserved. No part of this book may be used or reproduced in any manner without the written permission of the copyright owner except for the use of quotations in a book review.

To the Youth of Our Generation

Let's Speak Freely

(Dr. Muhammad Shahzad and Dr. Baland Iqbal)

Lament for the Motherland

The vultures sit upon my body—
Tearing apart every morsel of my flesh.

My eyes... the nest of my beautiful dreams,
My tongue... the mirror of pearl-like words,
My arms... the guarantors of dream-fulfilled visions,
My heart... where even the impossible found possibility.

And my soul—
It watches this entire scene unfold,
And wonders:

Was this entire spectacle—
(My corpse upon the feasting table of the bloodthirsty)
Simply for the pleasure
Of their ravenous indulgence?

(Himayat Ali Shair)

Preface

When Dr. Muhammad Shahzad told me that he wanted to speak candidly with me on some thorny subjects, I instinctively responded, "Of course, please do — but why do you feel the need?" To this he replied, "For the sake of the political and social awareness of Pakistan's younger generation."

According to him, the generation of Pakistani youth born after the 1980s has had its intellectual and critical faculties deliberately confined within certain limits by an exploitative class through calculated planning — so that they may always be easily manipulated for that class's own interests.

In his view, there are a number of fundamental topics — such as the difference between artificial and real democracy, secularism versus atheism, patriarchal social issues, extremist ideologies, mob mentalities, political maneuvers of dominant powers, the rights and limitations surrounding freedom of thought and expression, the political entanglement of religion and the state, the real meanings of superficial morality, the way the institution of marriage perpetuates racism and prejudice, and the role of real and artificial intelligence in human society.

He wanted me to speak openly on these matters so that the mental perspectives of our youth could gain greater depth and breadth — so they might become capable of criticism, discussion, and logical debate.

He said he would ask me five questions on each topic and hoped that I would respond with complete honesty. I found the idea of five questions quite appealing — for me, the number five is symbolic of the five daily prayers in Islam. It occurred to me that just as the number five holds sacred value in religion, perhaps it can hold a similar reverence in the social sciences — provided we respond to these questions with total truthfulness and sincerity, for the sake of enlightening the minds of the younger generation.

(Dr. Baland Iqbal)

The Significance of Questioning —
The Story of My Intellectual Odyssey

The first time I posed a question, people were incensed. The second time, they branded me disrespectful. But the third time I dared to ask, my father gently placed his hand on my shoulder and said, "Never be afraid to articulate the truth — questioning is your inherent right." That moment marked the genesis of my resistance, and silence became an anathema to me.

I hail from a society where questioning is perceived as a transgression, and the courage to question is deemed rebellion. However, within the confines of my home, my father taught me a different lesson — question faith, question tradition, question power. And persist in seeking answers until the truth emerges. This courage illuminated a new path for me, one where intellectual curiosity and social awareness converged.

My father's teachings instilled in me the bravery to ask bold questions, guiding me down a road where I could elevate both my intellectual and social awareness. His intellectual mentorship taught me that unless we question, we can never arrive at the truth. Following that path, I discovered the purpose of my life.

Both of my parents were highly educated and politically active, shaping not only my academic direction but also imbuing me with the confidence to engage with complex social and political issues. Their activism and deep social consciousness taught me that asking questions is not just a personal right — it is a collective responsibility.

During my college years, I co-founded a discussion platform with like-minded friends called "Charsadda Circles." It became a sanctuary where we discussed subjects often deemed forbidden in society, raising critical questions about politics, education, and social reform through an informal yet deeply thoughtful approach. Eventually, this circle evolved into an intellectual movement, joined by thousands of youth, encouraging them to think critically and question bravely.

These questions opened the doors of thought, helping us view the world through new perspectives. For us, questioning became an act of resistance — resistance against oppressive traditions and anti-democratic forces. Unsurprisingly, this didn't sit well with those whose power thrived on blind obedience, and we began receiving anonymous calls and death threats from 'intelligence' agencies. Nevertheless, we refused to be silenced and continued our struggle.

One day, during my final year of medical school, a former government minister visited my father, warning, "If your son doesn't stop asking these questions, it could affect his medical career. What if he's picked up during exams? A gold medalist today might fall far behind his peers tomorrow." My father, a man I proudly call my role model, smiled calmly and told me, "Keep asking questions. I'm here with you." That message became a challenge, testing my conviction. Yet, his unwavering support only strengthened my resolve, and I continued my academic journey while deepening my commitment to questioning and intellectual resistance.

The impact of my questions was profound, inspiring thousands of young people to join the movement. Charsadda Circles eventually transformed into Pukhtunkhwa Circles, a platform that gave voice to youth across the region, empowering them to ask questions and teaching them that questioning is not just a right — it's a responsibility.

Our conversations addressed deeper themes — social reform, democracy, and human rights. We challenged outdated traditions and authoritarian institutions, showing young people that through questions, knowledge expands, and a new kind of social consciousness begins to emerge.

During this time, Dr. Usman conducted PhD research on our movement, portraying our intellectual resistance as a grassroots struggle in informal settings. His research validated that asking *questions is not merely a right — it is an essential act that nurtures reason and intellectual freedom in every society.*

This journey was never just about questioning — it became a full-fledged movement, sparking societal transformation, academic research, and global recognition. Through this, we helped young minds awaken to reason, giving rise to new ideas, fresh perspectives, and progressive thought.

Today, I dedicate this book to the thousands of youth like me — those who long for truth and believe that thinking begins with questioning. On this intellectual journey, I am joined by my teacher and co-author, Baland Iqbal, whose words bring the light of wisdom to every page.

This book is not just an ideology — it is a mission: A mission to keep dialogue alive, to legitimize the act of questioning, and to inspire a generation of young people to think critically. For me, this book is a personal pledge — to express my thoughts freely and to show the world that questioning and illuminating the mind is not only our right but also our responsibility.

With the foundational teachings of my father and the support of mentors like Baland Iqbal, my intellectual journey found its voice. They gave deeper meaning to every question I asked. My life — and this book — serve as a reminder: It is through brave questions that progress is made. And it is through courageous thought that societies evolve.

(Dr. Muhammad Shahzad)

Dr. Muhammad Shahzad: A Beacon of Reform

"We should not become misologues, as people become misanthropes. There is no greater evil one can suffer than to hate reasonable discourse. Misology and misanthropy arise in the same way. Misanthropy comes when a man without knowledge or skill has placed great trust in someone and believes him to be altogether truthful, sound, and trustworthy; then, a short time afterwards he finds him to be wicked and unreliable, and then this happens in another case; when one has frequently had that experience, especially with those whom one believed to be one's closest friends, then, in the end, after many such blows, one comes to hate all men and to believe that no one is sound in any way at all."

(Plato, Five Dialogues: Euthyphro, Apology, Crito, Meno, Phaedo)

We are born and bred in a society that can be dubbed a "closed society"—one with little space for open dialogue or genuine discussion. While there may be superficial exchanges, they remain confined within the traditional straitjacket of dogmatic religious, sectarian, and pseudo-political frameworks. From mosques to temples, and from madrassas to maktabs, all institutions are subservient to predetermined socio-economic and political dogmas—whether divinely revealed or artificially imposed, overtly or covertly. These structures produce a warrior generation, conditioned to eliminate those who differ in thought and outlook. This militant generation is now surfacing in various forms, under different slogans and agendas, not only arresting societal progress but also playing a pivotal role in shaping and destabilizing governments and states across our region.

Dr. Muhammad Shahzad, a young medical doctor from the historic city of Pushkalavati (modern-day Charsadda)—the birthplace of the nonviolent leader Khan Abdul Ghaffar Khan, popularly known as Bacha Khan—is an energetic nationalist with a passion for knowledge and reform. Academically brilliant, he earned his MBBS with distinction (Gold Medal) and later pursued degrees in Political Science, Law, and International Relations as a private candidate. Currently, he is completing a Master's in Public Health and Epidemiology.

Beyond his academic achievements, Dr. Shahzad is an active member of various social organizations and intellectual forums. As General Secretary of Malgari Doctoran Pakhtunkhwa, he leads the province's progressive medical community with integrity. He also founded Pakhtunkhwa Circles, an influential intellectual movement fostering critical discourse among youth through study circles on science, history, philosophy, and politics.

More than just a physician, Dr. Shahzad is a reformist social worker dedicated to serving the downtrodden without expectation. As an active member of the Bacha Khan Research Center in Peshawar, he systematically organizes monthly study circles with structured critical discourse. His persuasive and articulate style of presentation evokes the traditional storytellers of Pakhtunkhwa, who had a masterful command over words and the ability to captivate their audience.

In our current socio-economic and political turmoil—where societal norms and values are shattered at all levels—the need for critical engagement with contemporary issues has never been more urgent. Amid rapid technological change, deepening inequalities, and global crises (from climate emergencies to political upheavals), this book emerges as a commitment to interrogating modernity, offering a multidisciplinary lens to examine the forces shaping our world.

The book is an anthology—a collection of dialogues between Dr. Muhammad Shahzad and Dr. Baland Iqbal—intended for open-minded youth in an academic, liberal, and secular environment. This collaborative effort represents a new beginning in a society gripped by conservatism, dogmatism, inertia, ignorance, illiteracy, sectarianism, extremism, and religious bigotry.

In classical literature, the purpose of dialogue is to argue. The five questions and answers between Dr. Shahzad and Dr. Baland Iqbal resemble the five daily prayers in Islam—a parallel drawn by Dr. Baland Iqbal. However, to me, Dr. Shahzad seems to invoke, consciously or unconsciously, the mythological significance of the number five.

In Greek mythology, the number five holds symbolic weight—Hesiod's Five Ages of Man (Golden, Silver, Bronze, Heroic, and Iron) categorizes distinct epochs of human history. In Persian mythology and Zoroastrianism, five carries profound meaning—linked to Sarosh Yazad (a divine entity governing obedience and the five senses), the division of the day, social structure, and the Gathas.

The current dialogue underscores the urgency of freeing minds from manufactured constraints. Only through critical thought can societies transcend artificial divides and reclaim agency. The youth must question, debate, and reimagine—because a mind unchained is the first step toward a society unchained.

The dialogues in this book unfold like a snowball, encompassing colonial intricacies, the fragmentation of Indian society, and ultimately, the partition of the subcontinent on communal lines. While this division temporarily satisfied the ruling elite, the dreams of Pakistan's founders and their supporters soon evaporated.

Dr. Baland Iqbal, in his responses, meticulously dissects the micro-level societal issues of our society and our country, weaving past and present in a logical, coherent manner.

At the end, Dr. Baland Iqbal stated,

"I believe, Shahzad that you and I are among these organic thinkers — engaged in an unending effort to examine and articulate these themes. We are not just discussing them but also working to shape *them into books—so that, in our own modest way, we can light a lamp of awareness and provide some guidance for the next generation."*

Dr. B. Iqbal last wordings reflect a profound commitment to intellectual and philosophical inquiry, as well as a desire to contribute meaningfully to the discourse on important themes for future generations. The mention of "organic thinkers" suggests a focus on natural, evolving thought processes rather than rigid or dogmatic approaches.

Last but not least I would like to say that the Muhajir elites from India imposed their own cultural norms and values on the nationalities living within the new geographical domain called Pakistan. Secondly, the Afghan Revolution of 1978, followed by the Soviet intervention in Afghanistan and the Islamic Revolution in Iran, severely dented the entire fabric of society and the state.

Professor Dr. Fazal-Ur-Rahim Marwat

Ex-VC Bacha Khan University Charsadda.
Director Bacha Khan Research Center
Pajagi Road Peshawar - Pakistan

Contents

- This mind must be prevented from functioning for twenty years.   21
- This mind must be afflicted with the disease of extremism.   39
- This mind must be herded like sheep.   53
- This mind must be kept under the illusion of democracy.   67
- This mind must be trapped in a tribal patriarchal mentality.   83
- This mind must be fed lies about secularism.   97
- This mind must be kept at the lowest level of moral superficiality.   113
- This mind must be distanced from genuine intelligence.   127
- This mind must be trapped in misconceptions about Islamophobia.   143
- This mind must be kept unaware of the reality of the marriage system.   155
- This mind must be confined within an artificial intelligence.   167
- This mind must be restricted from thinking and speaking freely.   177

To Free This Mind...

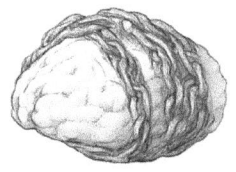

This mind must be prevented from functioning for twenty years

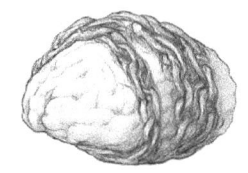

Dr. Muhammad Shahzad:

My first question for you, Doctor Iqbal, is about defining our society: how would you introduce our society? Is it a natural society, or is it an artificial one?

Dr. Baland Iqbal:

Shahzad, your question is very important. First, it is best to understand how human societies underwent social and political evolution. Then, by comparing that to biological evolution, we realize how Darwin's idea of "survival of the fittest" was shaped—and even altered—by social and political necessities. This is the major canon we can apply to our own society and analyze through a multidisciplinary lens.

See, as a result, a distinctly artificial social structure also emerged. Biological and social survival efforts have played the most crucial roles in shaping and nurturing human society. Whether "selection of the fittest" is biological or social, in both cases "genetic mutation" has been a fundamental factor. Because of humans' political and social endeavors to survive, a major "genetic drift" has taken place—we observe a unidirectional genetic flow, leading to the human species evolving into what we ultimately call Homo sapiens.

To illustrate, consider another animal species: the dog. What we call a dog is actually a wolf that, over centuries of evolution and mutation, transformed. Some wolves remained wolves, while others became dogs—no longer wild, but domesticated and beloved. Would anyone today keep a wolf as part of their family, raising it like a child?

Another important question: how have social factors influenced biological evolution differently in humans than in animals? In humans, we see that over time, the changes occurred primarily in the brain's "higher parts" or "Special Brain Centres." While the fundamental biological instincts—eating, drinking, reproduction, and survival—are similar to animals, human social instinct is fundamentally different due to brain structure. The human "Temporal Cerebral Relation" is far more advanced in function than that of any animal.

If you read Yuval Noah Harari's *A Brief History of Humankind*, which charts 3.5 million years of social and biological evolution, you see this clearly. He begins in the Stone Age and shows how temperature changes led to ice ages, shifting sea levels, and animal migrations. Large animals became extinct, smaller animals spread across continents and cross-pollinated into new species. Various human species—like chimpanzees, apes, *Homo neanderthalensis*, *Homo erectus*, *Homo rudolfensis*—spread to different regions, interbred for centuries, and eventually gave rise to modern Homo sapiens.

So, although *Homo sapiens* emerged through Natural Selection, social and political pressures introduced specific genetic mutations and flows, differentiating them from other animals into a completely distinct cultural being. As we move from the Old Stone Age to the Middle and Late Stone Ages, the concept becomes clearer. Roughly 10,000 years ago—around the Middle Stone Age—we see shifts toward organized agricultural societies. By 2,500–3,000 BC, we were in the Copper and Bronze Ages, with organized legal systems, welfare, and religion. What began in the Hunting Age became civilized and agricultural. Anthropologists like Lewis Henry Morgan and Auguste Comte tell us humans transition from metaphysical ignorance to proto-science to reflective thought and finally to a critical-conscious Era. Industrialization and modern science followed 1,500 years ago.

All of these changes stemmed from genetic drift, mutation, and change in response to environmental and social challenges. But human genetic drift was quite different from that of animals. Over time, Homo sapiens gained higher cognitive abilities: creation, imagination, cooperation, unification—capabilities no other species developed. This enabled them to build increasingly complex societies, from hunter-gatherers to industrial technology, driven by an advanced Temporal-Cerebral link unique to humans.

Yet these social changes weren't peaceful. They involved wars—tribal conflicts, conquest, bloodshed—violent struggles for survival and dominance. These violent processes also mutated human biology. The genetic drift and flow were driven by both natural and artificial processes, forging what we call modern human society. The original "natural" Homo sapiens mostly vanished, leaving behind mutated materials and their tools.

As we moved into the Computer Age, this Temporal-Cerebral link continued to evolve—differently in different regions—shaped by climate, culture, politics, and social experiences. Though anatomically similar, humans in different geographic groups developed unique cognitive and genetic traits across eras.

Understanding this process reveals a ruthless political and social ideology. A dominant human class has deliberately steered different human groups toward specific directions—an artificially constructed society. Here, Gramsci's *Theory of Hegemony* becomes crucial. It shows how societies—European, Asian, even Pakistani over the past 70–75 years—have been guided into particular political and social trajectories. Hegemony teaches us how public mentality can be shaped, just as animals are trained. An entire human society can thus be developed in a chosen direction.

Therefore, I believe it's essential—not just for political science students but for every citizen—to understand the *Theory of Hegemony* well.

Dr. Muhammad Shahzad:

Dr. Iqbal, how has this *hegemony* had an overarching impact on Pakistani society?

Dr. Baland Iqbal:

Certainly, Shahzad, this is an important topic. Let's begin by briefly exploring the background of this terminology. The socio-philosophical concept of *hegemony* is primarily associated with the Marxist philosopher Antonio Gramsci, who was born in 1891. Unfortunately, he lived a short life—he died in 1937 at the age of only 46. A large part of this short life—about twenty years—was spent in prison. Gramsci was fundamentally an *Ideological Marxist* and a staunch opponent of *Mussolini's Fascism*. When he was imprisoned, the judge made a now-famous remark about him:

"For twenty years we must stop this brain from functioning."

The intent was clear: to silence a mind whose brilliance was uncovering the mechanisms by which *dominating powers* control society. After spending eleven continuous years in prison, Gramsci fell seriously ill. He was transferred to a hospital, where he eventually died. After his death, thirty notebooks were recovered from his prison cell—comprising nearly 3,000 pages of his theories. These writings came to be known as the *Prison Notebooks*. They are now regarded as one of the most important *Post-Marxist Political Theories* of the 20th century and are considered an original contribution to political science. Gramsci's work aimed to demonstrate how *dominating powers* craft social behavior to maintain control over the state—how they construct an artificial social superstructure that appears, to the public, as a natural and authentic social order.

To understand why Gramsci thought this way, one must consider the historical context in which he lived—between the two World Wars. In 1917, the Russian Revolution occurred, bringing the *Bolsheviks* to power. Then, between 1939 and 1945, the world was engulfed by the Second World War. In 1947, the Chinese Revolution followed. The world subsequently split into two ideological blocs—Communist and Capitalist. Gramsci's theory posed a profound question: despite the initial success of the Communist revolutions, why did much of the world eventually become *Capitalist*?

His answer was that *Capitalist forces*, through sophisticated *political strategies*, created *dominating powers* that prevented the establishment of Communist states. According to Gramsci, the state is fundamentally based on economics, around which an organized structure forms. The *dominating power* divides this structure into two main components: one is the *Civil Society*, and the other comprises the military, judiciary, and legislature. The *Civil Society* includes institutions like universities, colleges, mosques, temples, churches, and media outlets. These together form a comprehensive social-political structure. The *dominating powers* utilize both spheres in a delicate balance.

Their central objective is to mentally condition the public to willingly offer *consent*. These powers train civil institutions to influence public opinion in such a way that people gladly accept the decisions made by the military, judiciary, and legislature—often even perceiving these decisions as being in their own best interest. This voluntary *consent* is what Gramsci defines as *hegemony*. He argued that until this *hegemony* is dismantled within a state, no revolution or new system can truly emerge. This is precisely why, despite the Communist revolutions, true Communist states failed to endure—because they were unable to break the prevailing *hegemony*. Capitalism persisted or reasserted itself.

During this time, Gramsci also introduced the term *Organic Intellectuals*. These are individuals who deeply understand this entire process and adopt a critical stance against it.

Now, as for your question about where this *hegemony* is visible in Pakistan—the answer is, it has been present in a consistent form since the country's very inception. Remember, before its creation, Pakistan was part of a British colony. That means a *dominating power*—the British—was already controlling the regions that would become Pakistan. What was the cultural landscape of the subcontinent before Partition? For centuries, it had been shaped by a syncretic culture—a harmonious coexistence of Hindus and Muslims who had lived together for 400–500 years.

But the British *dominating power* disrupted this equilibrium. Within the *civil society*, it sowed the seeds of *Hindu-Muslim antagonism*. This was a deliberate, fabricated *political narrative*—essentially a fraud—designed to manipulate hearts and minds in service of their own geopolitical strategy. In this way, the creation of Pakistan involved the deliberate construction of a complete socio-political structure. Artificial ideologies were fabricated, leaders were manufactured, and cultural differences—largely absent in the prior centuries—were exaggerated. Political concepts were employed to carve out space for the *two-nation theory*, ultimately dividing the Indian nation—a future Asian powerhouse—on the basis of religion and culture.

During this period, we see two types of political leaders. The *Non-organic Intellectuals* were those aligned with the *dominating powers*. These individuals were never imprisoned during the freedom struggle because they aided the agenda of division and promoted that ideology within *civil society*. The result was a catastrophic historical loss for Muslims—they were fragmented into weaker units, easily exploited by larger powers for political purposes.

On the other hand, the *organic intellectuals*—the real thinkers—opposed the two-nation theory. Among them were Obaidullah Sindhi, Maulana Abul Kalam Azad, Syed Hussain Ahmed Madani, even Maulana Maududi, and "Sarhadi Gandhi" Khan Abdul Ghaffar Khan. These great minds recognized the *hegemony* at play. They consistently rejected Partition. They warned that a manufactured scheme was unfolding—but the masses were steered toward a singular direction, and the outcome was exactly what the *dominating powers* had planned. India was divided, and Pakistan came into existence.

But the natural result was this: an unnatural state quickly fractured. Since its creation, Pakistan has remained under the control of those *dominating powers*, because it was made for that very purpose—to serve their strategic and geopolitical interests in the region. To that end, the British *dominating power* utilized a regiment of the Indian Army (from Punjab) that had always been loyal to them, which had, on numerous occasions, sided with the British against Indian revolutionaries during the freedom struggle. After Pakistan's creation, this same regiment established a *local establishment* aligned with major global powers and has maintained a sustained grip over the country ever since.

Now look at the consequences: an artificial social, political—even religious—culture is consistently shaped in a predetermined direction. Since its inception, Pakistan's *dominating establishment* has continuously reshaped the country's identity according to the instructions of *superpowers*. One moment it is General Zia-ul-Haq's "Islamic Pakistan," then it becomes General Musharraf's "Enlightened Pakistan." At times it is Bhutto's "Socialist Pakistan," then Nawaz Sharif's "Commercial Pakistan," then Imran Khan's

"Madina-style Pakistan," and at other times it transforms into "Communist Pakistan" under Chinese influence. One day it is "China-Pakistan brothers forever," the next day it's "Friend of America is a traitor"—only to turn back into "America's darling" again. At one point, jihad against Russia promises heaven; another time, without Russia, our economic paradise is doomed.

To produce this sort of *consent* or collective *conformity*, *dominating powers* always rely on the tools of *civil society*—educational institutions, media industries, and charismatic political, religious, and social leaders. In return, the public willingly signs the *contract*—cheering at political rallies, pledging allegiance to these leaders. This entire *hegemony* process reconditions the public every five years.

In this process, TV media, social media, dramas, seminars, school and college curriculums, and nowadays TikTok videos, YouTube channels, and WhatsApp forwards are all employed to shape public opinion. Mountains of unverified, false news are manufactured, inundating public consciousness. The fraud is so extensive that even the truth begins to doubt itself. Once this psychological engineering is complete, elections are arranged, real and fake votes are cast, and the *dominating power* installs a new regime to continue its reign.

Meanwhile, the public remains mentally paralyzed, as most people naturally view complex realities in a shallow, one-dimensional way. They are conditioned never to perceive the other sides of the matchbox, because their minds are never trained for three-dimensional understanding.

Through the lens of Gramsci's *hegemony* theory, one can clearly comprehend Pakistan's foundational idea, its construction, and the socio-political architecture it has evolved into. It reveals how today's fragmented, constructed, or fractured Pakistan came into being.

Shahzad, the only way for Pakistan to escape this state is by breaking the *hegemony*—this psychological and cultural *consent*. But this is nearly impossible, because the *dominating powers* have deliberately created a society devoid of critical intellect and independent consciousness. These powers hold complete control over the most influential tools of *civil society*: schools, colleges, mosques, media, newspapers, as well as the coercive apparatuses—military, police, judiciary, and bureaucracy. This makes any meaningful transformation in Pakistan virtually impossible.

Dr. Muhammad Shahzad:

What is your opinion about Pakistan? Would you consider Pakistan to be a truly religious society?

Dr. Baland Iqbal:

Shahzad, rather than jumping straight into the debate of whether Pakistan is truly a religious society, we must first understand the *Intellectual Value* of religion and its delicate relationship with human psychology. We must also examine the social and civilizational roles religion has played throughout history, and assess whether those roles have ultimately benefited or harmed society.

If we look at the evolutionary development of religion, we find that *Organized Religion* emerged around two to two-and-a-half thousand years ago, during the agricultural eras. It is evident that early human societies had some positive intentions behind the formation of religion. Foremost among these was likely the effort to give human life a sense of meaning, or to unify society under a common moral vision—creating a *Unified* social identity. Religion served to foster a healthy sense of conscience among people, regulate individual and collective behavior, and facilitate positive social transformation. By the standards of those times, these efforts were largely successful.

Now, when it comes to individual matters of human behavior, it's difficult—if not impossible—to judge or analyze them through the so-called *Universal Principles* of religious ethics. That's because each person's moral compass tends to differ, shaped by unique variables such as consciousness, upbringing, education, cultural norms, and social practices. And when we talk about groups—large numbers of religious people—we encounter significant bias in thought rooted in their particular beliefs. Yet we lack any reliable tool or formula that could measure or quantify this *Bias Mode*, such that we might claim all individuals within it share identical religious values.

So, in simpler terms, the point is this: we encounter such a wide variety of shifting religious and non-religious moral standards in society that it's easier to classify individuals, rather than entire societies, as either religious or non-religious.

However, one thing can be said with relative clarity: individuals—whether men or women—tend to be religious either *Culturally* or *Spiritually Religious*. By *Culturally Religious*, I mean someone who adopts religious rituals and customs as a form of *Cultural Security*. Now, the question is—why do they do this? On the surface, it appears that doing so brings ease to their lives, gives them a sense of identity within a particular community, instills pride, and generates a kind of ego—something that is a crucial element in personal psychology. This lifestyle also comes with social advantages, and the collective opinion formed in their favor can resolve many of their practical problems.

On the other hand, those who are *Spiritually Religious* genuinely internalize the spiritual teachings of their religion, making them a part of their psychological framework. Not only do they live by these teachings, but they also actively try to convince others of them.

Now Shahzad, if you consider these two modes—*Cultural* and *Spiritual* religiosity—and apply them at the individual level across Pakistan's 250 million people, how would the proportions of each group ethically validate their religious identities? If you feel it's appropriate, perhaps this proportional analysis could help you decide whether a Pakistani individual—or society as a whole—deserves to be called religious or non-religious.

As far as Pakistan is concerned, we know it is home to numerous religious sects, and individuals typically adhere to the *spiritual* or *cultural* aspects—and values—of only their own *sect*. If we look at North America, for instance, I believe people there are largely *Culturally Religious*; they follow *Christian Cultural Values*. Now the question arises: if they are not *Spiritually Religious* or even religious at all, why do they exhibit better moral behavior?

In my view, the answer lies in the pressure exerted by the legal system—nothing more. I believe human beings, by nature, are cultural creatures, inclined toward adhering to ethical principles. They don't necessarily need the rigid commandments of religion to do so. In past eras, where humans were more primitive or tribal, the authority of religion—and the very notion of a God—may have helped civilize them. But by the 21st century, the average human being has evolved to such an extent that even *Atheists* are often found to be more morally upright than religious individuals.

Of course, there are always problematic individuals in any society, but this often relates more to the economic development and social structure of that society. Generally speaking, people tend to be good—they help each other, look out for one another—and they do this without necessarily invoking religion.

Now, in Pakistani society, religion is so visibly present—there are constant religious discussions, public gatherings, religious programming on the media, mosques and madrassas scattered throughout towns and neighborhoods, and the sound of the call to prayer echoes in the air—that it gives the *illusion* of being a religious society. But rather than judging based on this visible *social structure*, we should analyze the balance and distinction between *Spiritual* and *Cultural Religion* to make an informed judgment.

The truth is, we frequently witness that as soon as a prayer ends in a mosque, what immediately follows outside is vulgar abuse, violence, theft, and bribery. A person may wear a cap on his head and a scarf on her face, but inside, there's a wild animal waiting to break free. It's as though the cap and scarf are feeble attempts to restrain something far more unruly. Even after a full day of worship, that inner self-centered being remains fully active, selfishly focused only on personal interest, carrying numerous ethical flaws that can harm society at large.

Given this, we must ask: what label should we assign to such individuals or societies? Are they *Culturally Religious* or *Spiritually Religious*? And this leads to deeper questions. At what point did the historical balance between religion and society begin to break down? Are religion and morality even judged by the same standards—or are they entirely unrelated?

There's also the hard question: can we actually separate religion from politics? Or did religion ever have a philosophically strong enough foundation to bear the weight of moral responsibility in the first place? Because the bitter truth is, despite centuries of political reinforcement, religion has failed to bring about collective intellectual progress in humanity.

To be clear, this isn't a critique of Islam alone—it's a broader issue across religious societies around the world. That's why I say the categorization of societies as religious or non-religious is ultimately *Arbitrary*. They cannot be neatly boxed into either label.

Shahzad, I believe that in the sociocultural and economic framework of 21st-century globalization, religion, language, and customs are gradually merging. Within the next fifty years—or perhaps even the next ten to twenty—a *Unified* social structure will begin to emerge. This structure will be healthier and more balanced than any previous model of human civilization. The traditional concepts of nationalism and religion will weaken, and the distances between people will begin to shrink. As different nations and religions come together, tolerance will increase, racial and ethnic divisions will diminish, and societies will gradually move toward a state free from polarization.

Dr. Muhammad Shahzad:

You just mentioned that the classification of a society as religious or non-religious is an arbitrary division that depends on the discretion of the classifier. So, can we say the same about any kind of social classification, or are there cases where we can reasonably express a different opinion? For example, can we introduce India as a democratic society? Or Europe as a secular place? Or North America as a Western society? And Pakistan as an Eastern society? Or Saudi Arabia as a fascist society?

Dr. Baland Iqbal:

Shahzad, when it comes to questions like whether we are an Eastern society, or North America is a Western society, or Europe is a secular society, or Saudi Arabia is a fascist society, or whether India is a democratic society—if we look at it truthfully, such classifications appear to be more academic than real. In today's era, such distinctions are no longer viable because this is the age of economic imperialism. In the past, political imperialist governments used to rule other nations by force, but the world has changed now.

When we say a country is Eastern or Western, or religious or non-religious, we're often referring to its culture. But when we try to make geographical distinctions based on political ideologies, a clear division becomes difficult. For example, if a state like India claims to be democratic, it must also strive to prove itself so and meet the criteria it asserts. Or if Saudi Arabia is a fascist state, then its effects must visibly trickle down from the government to the people.

Today, we live in a global society—one where the scales of trade, exchange, and political influence have expanded immensely. From the perspective of technology, culture, or finance, the dominance of the West is clearly visible. Yes, it's true that alongside the West, countries like China and India are also emerging as major powers, and we see the influence of Japan and South Korea as well.

But when it comes to Europe and North America, they are not only controlling developing countries through financial institutions like the World Bank and IMF, but also playing a major role through cultural imperialism. For example, franchises of McDonald's and Coca-Cola are visible across the globe. Likewise, Western ideological concepts—such as the idea of individual freedom or the separation of religion from government—are spreading throughout society.

In reality, economic imperialism and cultural influence have always been intertwined, because cultural absorption or diffusion plays a backbone role in economic expansion.

Now, the question is: if China or India emerges as a powerhouse in South and Central Asia in the coming days, will they be able to spread their culture the way Western nations have? A foundational element in any culture's structure is its language or linguistic value. For instance, American dramas and soap operas are seen everywhere in the media. But can Latin American soaps attain that kind of global reach?

Similarly, how much potential do languages like Chinese, Korean, or India's Sanskrit have in this context? Also, how much academic or scientific work has been done in these languages? To what extent have these nations managed to extend their presence on the internet or social media?

Most importantly, how attractive are these countries' immigration systems to people from other nations? Have they offered equal opportunities for others to live, settle, and do business freely in their societies? There's no denying that the English language, being a global language, has played a crucial role in the economic and cultural advancement of Western nations. This is also due in large part to the language's inherent openness. Compared to other languages, English grammar, its capacity to integrate words from other languages, its literature, scientific terminology, and adaptability to future needs all point to its exceptional breadth and versatility. This is why its spread has contributed to economic development.

From this perspective, we can say that even fascist, religious, or communist societies will eventually need to coexist with liberal democratic societies and other orthodox, tribal, or religious groups if they wish to enter the modern global economic world. So, while such arbitrary classifications may be valid academically or for the sake of introduction, in reality, the values of societies are determined not just by economics but also by culture, language, customs, and natural adaptability.

Dr. Muhammad Shahzad:

Doctor Iqbal, when we become aware of these truths, what should our response be as social individuals? How can we, as natural social beings, maintain our balance in an artificial society?

Dr. Baland Iqbal:

Look, Shahzad, we must not forget that we are riding in a cultural cart that essentially runs on four wheels. The first is technological invasion; the second is the control of financial institutions over our capitalist economy; the third is political and religious extremism or social polarization; and the fourth is the threats of global warming and nuclear invasion. Clearly, the steering of the cart is what helps us maintain balance in our natural life.

All around us is a naturally evolved cultural world in which we must steer our cart through the flow of life with balance. These four wheels of our cart may appear separate and distinct, but in truth, they are all connected to the same engine.

For instance, global warming is directly linked to capitalist economies and industrialization. Or political and religious fundamentalism is one of the strongest weapons used by dominant state powers. It's crucial to observe and analyze how these factors are disturbing the balance or pace of our cart's progress—because our future generations, too, will ride on this same cultural cart. If we do not drive it wisely or throw it off balance, our children will only inherit a life full of problems.

Look, Shahzad, dominant or controlling powers of the state have always wanted our life's cart to run according to their will. Their goal has always been to sit in the driver's seat. To achieve this, they'll slow down or accelerate whichever wheel suits their needs to ensure the direction favors only them. For this, they employ the theory of hegemony, making us feel as though we are living our lives freely, when in fact we're unconsciously moving in directions set by them.

We need to be aware of the pros and cons of such directions. For example, we must recognize the benefits of technology—it improves our quality of life, enhances communication, brings comfort, provides access to information, and improves healthcare. But at the same time, technology increases social isolation and reduces the value of human workers.

Similarly, while the capitalist system promotes scientific innovation, freedom, and business opportunities, it also fosters political monopoly, further divides society into social classes, enriches the wealthy, and pushes the poor into deeper poverty. It increases social disparities.

In the same way, globalization—while spreading information and technology and developing a moderate culture—also spreads global infections. In short, we must make every effort to keep the cart of our natural cultural life balanced.

Look, Shahzad, I believe that every person only gets one chance at life. It's up to us whether we steer this social cart with balance toward success, or, due to ignorance, push it in a direction that causes severe harm and problems for our future generations.

It is our moral responsibility to make informed and balanced political, social, and economic decisions so that we do not have to face shame before the generations to come.

This mind must be afflicted with the disease of extremism

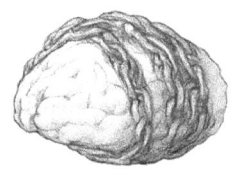

Dr. Muhammad Shahzad:

Dr. Iqbal, unfortunately, intellectual polarization in our society has increased significantly. What is your opinion on this matter?

Dr. Baland Iqbal:

Shahzad, polarization does not simply mean that there are two different groups or two different individuals with differing opinions. People's opinions can differ, and this difference is entirely natural. It actually reflects the diversity of any society. This diversity is what fundamentally constitutes the real structure of democracy; without it, the very idea of an individual's identity would cease to exist. In other words, having an ideology is a basic social right of any person.

However, Shahzad, polarization is a completely different phenomenon. During polarization, two groups or individuals come to be in absolute opposition to one another. They not only disagree, but they also hold a blind faith that their opposing group is entirely wrong and on a sinful path. They believe that their opponents are not only politically, philosophically, or religiously misguided, but also morally wrong. For them, it is a settled opinion that there is no possibility of improvement in the other side—they are utterly undeserving of being right, and are entirely on a path of sin.

Shahzad, I see the core of polarization closely tied to political issues. It seems to me that the kind of political impression our current politicians create in society due to their selfishness might succeed temporarily, but historically, the overall impact will be very damaging. The result will be a more ailing society. It is even possible that such conditions might lead to a civil war atmosphere, where people could go as far as shedding each other's blood. The historical figures from whom these politicians have learned or read about this style of politics are no longer alive. They have no idea how much damage humanity has suffered and how many problems the world now faces after their passing.

In contemporary times, the key factors driving polarization include charismatic yet narcissistic political leaders, their extremist thinking, the role of the media—especially print, electronic, and social media—and, importantly, the role of national and international establishments. The political use of religious ideologies, especially extremist interpretations, acts like pouring fuel on a fire.

Whenever we discuss polarization, we must not forget the role of populist leaders or political parties who show their prowess in many ways on the political stage, and whose influence is visible everywhere. For example, the late Venezuelan President Hugo Chávez in Latin America, or the political developments in Spain and Greece under past governments. These are examples from the left side of the political spectrum. On the right-wing side, one prominent name is Donald Trump. Others include Hungary's Viktor Orbán, France's Marine Le Pen, and many more who engage in sensational politics, constantly striving to stay in the media spotlight. In Greece, for instance, anti-immigrant political slogans were heavily exploited. Another aspect of this kind of politics is a strong authoritarian streak.

Recently, I briefly studied a book by Dr. Moffitt titled *Global Rise of Populism*. It provides examples of how this type of politics has surged over the past twenty-five to thirty years. It explains tactics and narratives used by leaders like Filipino President Duterte and Donald Trump, such as anti-intellectualism, anti-elite sentiments, and spreading various forms of negativity. Democracy, which is already established worldwide, is portrayed as a complicated system. Similar examples can be found almost everywhere—for instance, Narendra Modi in India, Jarosław Kaczyński in Poland, and Tayyip Erdogan in Turkey. These leaders are highly popular and powerful; they influence elections, operate through media industries, play roles on social media, and speak against the judiciary when it opposes t heir political ambitions. Their effect is to dismantle moderation and tolerance in society, giving rise to religious extremism and radicalism, which are then further polarized and exploited.

In Pakistan, there are several politicians whom you can consider responsible for polarization. You can observe how they chant slogans against their political opponents, make fun of them, produce various cartoons, overlay different kinds of background voices to prevent the public from taking them seriously, and even mock their personal and family lives. This creates an atmosphere of hatred, anger, and abuse, which naturally results in a deeply uncivil environment. Society easily divides into many parts. The situation deteriorates so much that even families split due to political ideologies; family members following different leaders refuse to maintain relationships or marry into each other's families. Similarly, families supporting different political views fail to maintain business relations. Thus, society fractures into numerous factions, and unfortunately, this atmosphere is increasingly visible across Pakistan due to recent political activities.

Dr. Muhammad Shahzad:

Sir, you just used the term "religious fundamentalism." Here, I would like to ask my second question: What are the psychological factors behind religious extremism? How does this mindset develop and take shape among the general public?

Dr. Baland Iqbal:

Certainly. Religious fundamentalism has several key features that we must understand, especially how this extremist mindset alters our general thinking. Religious and political polarization operate through more or less similar mechanisms.

From a psychological perspective, the most important element is the creation of a biased, "one-sided" (unidirectional) inclination, which we call dualistic thinking. Populist politicians deliberately exploit this. Their aim is to create extreme division, categorizing society into a stark black-and-white or binary division: for example, "We are good and righteous people, and you are bad and evil." Society is thus divided into right and wrong people—"us versus them"—with an irreconcilable gap between the two. There is almost no space between these boundaries for dialogue or reason. There is no "middle shade" that can blend these opposing colors to foster reconciliation. Instead, it is a black-and-white worldview filled only with distance, hatred, and enmity. This is the dualistic form of political extremism, which populist politicians adopt using techniques borrowed from religious fundamentalism.

Another major aspect I observe in this psychology is extreme paranoia—deep suspicion and mistrust of the other side. There is anger, aggression, and a constant smoldering hostility between them, like a burning fire in their hearts. The gap between them is vast and filled entirely with hatred.

Thirdly, in psychology, this situation often involves what we call "delusion" or irrational thinking. In religious thought, for example, this may manifest as a belief that we are living in a "corrupt age" (such as the Hindu mythological Kali Yuga), which will eventually end, giving rise to a new world, a new life, or a new society. These beliefs are disconnected from earthly realities.

The fourth thing you will notice, which is particularly striking, is that whether religious or political fundamentalist leaders, they share a common trait: they have a cult-like charismatic personality. Such leaders psychologically control their followers' minds. Their followers become possessed by them. If the leader says, "Sit down," the entire crowd sits; if he says, "Stand up," they all stand; if he says, "Clap together," they start clapping; if he says, "Follow me," the masses follow in lines like drones and zombies, like robots without thinking.

Followers of these political and religious leaders never question what kind of harm might result from these actions. They lose the capacity for critical thought and reasoning about whether the path the leader is taking them on is correct or not. They never ask themselves whether the leader himself might be doomed and might lead them all to ruin. There is no rational thought process available here.

The fourth important aspect I call "total conversion"—complete transformation. As soon as people join such extremist religious or political fundamentalist groups, they completely change. Perhaps a person was part of a less extreme political or religious group before, but upon joining a fundamentalist group, they transform entirely. As they say, they become "political jihadis," willing to die and kill, even ready to set the entire country on fire.

Dr. Muhammad Shahzad:

Continuing this discussion, Sir, my third question to you is: How has religious fundamentalism hijacked our minds? Generally speaking, is fundamentalism—whether religious or political—a mental illness?

Dr. Baland Iqbal:

Shahzad, you surely know that religion broadly presents us with two types of practices. One shows a certain moderation, softness, or balance, which I believe is somewhat necessary for mental peace, psychological health, and disciplining personal life. However, religious fundamentalism or extremism actually begins with a firm, rigid faith—an unshakable belief that there is an absolute, supreme authority in which everyone must have faith; or else, a strict blind faith in revealed scriptures and religious leaders. This rigid belief in texts—meaning the revealed scriptures and religious authorities—is precisely what triggers the problems of fundamentalism. Because fundamentalism challenges the understanding, scientific evidence, and rationality of ordinary people—or rather, non-religious ways of thinking constantly challenge the blind faith of fundamentalists—creating ongoing stress.

Now you ask, is fundamentalism a mental illness? I believe it is not a disease or pathology, but rather a mental germ or a mental parasite. This mental parasite affects the host it infects—it makes the host ill but does not completely kill it, because its own problem or plan is survival and proliferation. Unlike a typical parasite that invades and kills the body or brain, this parasite changes the infected person so profoundly that their temperament, thinking, and overall personality radically transform. The survival of this mental parasite depends on the life of its host because to multiply and convert a critical mind into a non-critical one, it requires a living host.

Now, how do we recognize or diagnose this? The diagnosis is essentially in reverse—if a person has undergone ideological brainwashing by fundamentalism, then we must go against that change and observe during their rehabilitation how their mind was initially affected, how their cognitive faculties were impaired.

Now, how does this parasite cause disease or produce the effects of fundamentalism? Just as a virus or bacteria attacks the biological human body or brain, this parasite acts similarly. When a bacteria or virus enters a body, its genes integrate into the genetic pool and replicate repeatedly. It starts releasing copies of itself. A good example of this is Richard Dawkins' 1976 book *The Selfish Gene*, where he introduced the concept of the "meme," a mental analogue of a gene that spreads culture. He explained how memes enter the "behavior pool" of the human brain, multiply, and spread throughout society, causing uniform behaviors. Here, the topic is religious fundamentalism and how entire societies fall victim to religious extremism. If this cultural gene is strong, it rapidly takes control over the whole society; if weak, it dies out after some time. This is very much like Darwin's theory of "survival of the fittest."

Now, if we connect this with concepts like fear and greed, we understand how religion initially enters the human mind. When a child grows, their mental and intellectual faculties develop. As they grow older, they begin to think about their future, develop a sense of morality and ethics. But when they realize their parents, siblings, and eventually themselves will die, anxiety arises. Religious beliefs offer psychological relief by providing an illusory concept of life after death. This is a major reason, but besides this, there is a whole psychological process that helps multiply religious culture by spreading its parasitic structure. In this regard, Daniel Dennett's book *The Mind and The Brain* explains how a brain becomes an artificial "artifact"—instead of a natural seat of thoughts and ideas, it becomes a container for religious concepts. This forms a permanent residence for religious ideology, where the mind no longer controls the brain, but the brain starts controlling the mind. The brain's natural function changes, causing the mind to work in a specific direction. The ideologies that emerge steer the mind into a particular framework. The memes producing cultural genes then undergo mutation, develop copies, and from these copies arise various subtypes, variants, or versions. Some variants are mild or moderate, while others are extremist or fundamentalist. For example, Christianity and Islam each have a large intellectual base that is mild in temperament—focusing on moral codes, ethics, psychological peace, and harmony. But alongside them, there are variants that are extremist and produce delusional thinking, leading to serious problems for society.

We can easily compare this to a computer infected by a Trojan virus. Just like a Trojan virus infects a computer, downloads itself into the software, and releases millions of copies, cultural genes—memes—behave similarly. For instance, people flock to temples, churches, or mosques, and in such a mental atmosphere, they accept these as truths and stick to them blindly. They practice these without much thought and often try to spread them throughout society. This process leads to the spread of a particular culture in society. For example, Christian fundamentalism has a distinct parasitic psychology. We call this "magical thinking"—a type of thinking disconnected from reality. This thinking spreads in fundamentalism as well. Psychologists and neurologists say this is a very powerful kind of thinking because it can accept any explanation, respond to any argument, and operates with a strong intuitive or instinctive attitude—an "I am right" mindset—lacking analytical or critical thinking. Above all, it involves a strong denial, especially of science. Since science is based on sensory observations, experiments, and specific hypotheses, fundamentalism rejects science outright. This rejection is necessary because objective truth would otherwise challenge religious fundamentalism and create existential problems for it.

Now, we should think about how to stop this self-replicative process—how to eliminate or at least reduce fundamentalism. The only way is to understand the entire fundamentalist ideology or mental inclination as a computerized biological system. Once we grasp this analogy, we will understand how brainwashing happens, how this mental parasite or virus spreads, and by explaining this to ordinary people, the intensity of fundamentalism will likely diminish.

Dr. Muhammad Shahzad:

Mr. Iqbal, social polarization and religious extremism are increasingly becoming global problems. What are your thoughts on this?

Dr. Baland Iqbal:

Look, Shahzad, Gandhi once said, "Those who think religion and politics are not connected neither understand religion nor politics." The truth is that religion and politics are deeply intertwined. Just recently, I was reading a 2012 research study from the United States that highlights the religious and political divisions in American society and how different communities support Republicans or Democrats. For example, in the Church of the Nazarene, 63% of people tend to support Republicans; similarly, 64% in Baptist churches, 65% in Presbyterian churches, and 75% in the Church of Christ favor Republicans. On the other hand, in areas where Muslims constitute 62%, Hindus 69%, or where African Christian churches exist, people tend to support Democrats. This division along religious lines translates into political affiliations.

Similarly, in India, since the rise of the Hindutva political movement, we have witnessed comparable trends. Vinayak Damodar Savarkar's famous 1923 book "Hindutva" framed Hindu nationalism not as a matter of geography but of civilization and culture, opposing Gandhi and Nehru's secular ideology. The result was the formation of a militant political party, the RSS, and gradually, what was once considered a great secular state transformed into a Hindu nationalist state. Since Narendra Modi's government came to power in 2014, India's political climate has changed significantly, not only causing political instability but also affecting its social and cultural image worldwide.

In Pakistan, the role of political parties and the establishment is no secret. Everyone knows that religious extremist groups have been trained behind political and military alliances, resulting in sectarian divisions among Shia, Sunni, Wahhabi, Deobandi, and Ahmadi factions. In Europe too, similar phenomena can be observed—whether in Brazil, Colombia, Bangladesh, Indonesia, Kenya, Poland, or Turkey—these patterns repeat themselves. A deeper look reveals similar political statuses and economic structures, with common political practices.

For example, polarization growth patterns in Kenya, Colombia, and Poland are almost identical. Jarosław Kaczyński in Poland utilized social media extensively, as did Tayyip Erdoğan in Turkey, who created a tense atmosphere against his opponents. Their main aim was electoral success. They portray their political opponents as demons to the public, often undermining democratic institutions. They exploit divisive issues that galvanize their voter base—for instance, anti-abortion slogans in Poland or anti-immigrant rhetoric in Italy.

This entire "industry" functions similarly worldwide, heavily using social media for anti-democratic tactics. They generate emotional reactions that fuel extremist behaviors and lead to social polarization. A good question here is: what role does the economy play? I'm not certain, but it might be significant. In India, for example, when the middle class became stronger, Hindu nationalism grew more intense. We should investigate what internal link exists between these developments. Corruption also plays a role; studies show that reducing corruption reduces polarization. Reducing favoritism, patronage, nepotism, and cronyism is crucial because these behaviors fuel division.

In all these societies, the institution most damaged by polarization is democracy itself, followed by the judiciary. Populist leaders developing polarization first attempt to delegitimize the judiciary to appoint their preferred people to government positions who will rule in their favor. In presidential systems, the president often prioritizes the political party over national issues. Consequently, societal balance and tolerance break down, and essential unity disappears. If polarization intensifies, society falls into anarchy, human rights abuses rise, hate crimes increase, political unrest spreads, and ultimately, civil war becomes a risk.

We have seen these patterns in India in recent years, frequently in Pakistan, in Poland, and in the U.S. since Donald Trump's presidency.

Dr. Muhammad Shahzad:

Dr. Iqbal, this is my last, fifth question: how can we reduce or eliminate this polarization?

Dr. Baland Iqbal:

Look, Shahzad, the key is dialogue—which is what we are doing right now. To reduce polarization, the importance of dialogue and sustained effort to maintain it cannot be overstated. Media reform is crucial, and even more so, national and international cooperation is needed, where political institutions come together seriously to curb these issues. Society's survival depends on preventing polarization.

Regarding institutional reform, we must consider decentralizing political systems and revising electoral laws. For instance, in 2016, the U.S. General Assembly passed a new law for the electoral system called "Ranked Choice Voting," aiming to discourage negative campaigning between political parties. Similarly, India recently enacted stringent laws against political violence and riots.

Regarding political leaders, examples abound: Lenin Moreno, former president of Ecuador, successfully campaigned on an anti-polarization platform, uniting people and winning elections. In Turkey, the 2019 mayoral candidate in Istanbul opposed the political and social divisions and also won. Such examples show that media reform, institutional change, and national/international policies are important.

However, most importantly, *we* as individuals have a role. We should reflect: do we seriously consider opposing opinions? How many of us watch TV channels that challenge our political views? How many blindly like and share polarizing comments on social media, encouraging such behavior? We ourselves become part of this chain. We often avoid open dialogue about such material and fail to criticize why hateful, divisive propaganda repeatedly appears on social media and why we accept it. Are we unwittingly part of this herd mentality or blind loyalty? Are we unknowingly perpetuating this social trend? Are we complicit in increasing polarization?

That is the most important question: as responsible citizens in these difficult times, what role should we play? Only then can we discuss further measures and genuinely strive to reduce or eliminate polarization from society.

This mind must be herded like sheep

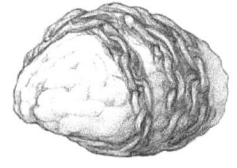

Dr. Muhammad Shahzad:

Dr. Iqbal, what exactly is meant by "herd mentality"? Is it a natural instinct found in humans similar to that of animals?

Dr. Baland Iqbal:

Shahzad, this is a very important topic, but unfortunately, such discussions are almost entirely absent from our universities and academic institutions. Rarely do we find even a single scholarly conversation addressing this issue.

We had recently tried to explore how we, as individuals and as a society, have been pushed—from religious fundamentalism to political extremism—through a deliberate and strategic process. Our society has been socially polarized and fragmented under a well-orchestrated plan. Unfortunately, at neither the Master's nor the Bachelor's level in our educational institutions will you find any reference to Sigmund Freud's *Civilization and Its Discontents*, a book that could help us understand the psychological development of individuals and society in a specific direction. Nor will you find any analysis of Pakistani society over the past eighty years through the lens of Antonio Gramsci's *Theory of Hegemony*. We lack any impartial, critical analysis to help us understand how society or the individual has been ideologically manipulated and for what sinister purposes.

Instead, the prevailing approach seems to be to lock young minds inside boxes, nesting their heads with ideas based on specific religious and social slogans. These hatch the stale, centuries-old repetitions of thought, giving birth to minds that are intellectually malnourished yet considered "mature." What's worse is that this process doesn't stop there—such backwardness and traditionalism are even celebrated. This is why a generation has emerged, brainwashed by motivational speakers like Qasim Ali Shah, Zakir Naik, and Tariq Jamil. The blind devotion cultivated by their rhetorical influence has produced a mediocre generation lacking in intellect and critical thought.

And if you try to discuss these issues in a modern, critical framework or attempt any analytical engagement, you'll likely be dismissed, insulted, or labeled negatively and pushed to the margins.

But this issue isn't unique to Pakistan. A similar scenario is unfolding in India. The point is, a specific form of intellectual decay surrounds us on all sides. Sadly, all that's growing is more grass for the same cattle. As a result, genuine social or intellectual transformation remains nearly nonexistent.

Now, regarding instinct: this is not a uniquely "human" instinct at all. Rather, it is an entirely animalistic trait found in sheep and other herd animals. It refers to a social thought process akin to a flock of sheep. It's the phenomenon of large groups of people who are physically together but not mentally coordinated. In English, this is often referred to as *sheeple behaviour*—a fusion of "sheep" and "people"—meaning behaviour that is indistinguishably shared between humans and animals. It is rooted in animal instincts.

Imagine a body composed of parts from different people—one person's hand, another's leg, someone else's torso and chest—together but lacking coordination. You'll find countless human examples of this. Like the flocks of sheep and herds of cattle, or swarms of birds, or lines of ants—human society often mimics the same formations.

You can observe this behaviour in public strikes, spontaneous reactions to sudden market crashes, or anywhere large groups act in unison without rational analysis. For instance, when someone fires into a flock of birds, each bird instinctively flies toward the centre of the flock to protect itself. Though this act is selfishly motivated for self-preservation, it appears—especially from a distance—as if all the birds are flying in coordinated harmony. In reality, they are not mentally connected; they are simply copying each other. That's *sheeple* behaviour.

Whether it's fashion, following a leader because others do, or embracing an ideology simply because it's popular—this is the same form of irrational mimicry. It is a type of animal-like craziness, a primitive behaviour pattern that has only minimally evolved in humans.

Dr. Muhammad Shahzad:

Sir, could you elaborate on the biological or scientific processes behind herd mentality?

Dr. Baland Iqbal:

Shahzad, there are several hypotheses in this regard. For example, Professor Vasily Klucharev of the University of Basel in Switzerland posits that dopamine plays a crucial role here. Dopamine, a neurotransmitter associated with the prefrontal cortex—the region of the brain involved in decision-making—is released during various situations, including life-threatening ones. It functions as a life-saving mechanism.

When you're among a crowd, dopamine is released normally because your brain perceives safety in numbers. However, when you deviate from crowd behaviour, dopamine is released more intensely, urging you—based on animal instinct—to conform for the sake of survival.

The brain starts sending messages that suggest your differing opinion is unsafe or incorrect, prompting a correction toward group consensus. This tendency has developed over centuries of evolutionary processes. The brain, bypassing social consciousness, reacts purely based on biological instinct—just as it would in other animals.

Kucherov demonstrated this in experiments where, using magnetic stimulation to reduce dopamine release in social settings, participants resisted conforming to group opinion. Conversely, in Denmark, a reverse experiment using dopamine injections showed that participants more easily aligned with group opinion.

Anatomical evidence also supports this: intellectuals, who tend to think independently and resist crowd mentality, generally have smaller prefrontal cortices, leading to less dopamine release.

This biological research provides a partial scientific explanation of herd behaviour. For psychological insights, we must turn to Sigmund Freud. In *Totem and Taboo* (1912) and *Group Psychology and the Analysis of the Ego*, Freud introduced concepts like the "ego ideal" and "libidinal dynamics," analyzing how an individual's ego adapts by idealizing that of the group. He emphasized internal psychological realities, but also acknowledged the importance of external ones—such as the "Great Man Syndrome" and the impact of social dynamics.

Further, in *Civilization and Its Discontents* and *Moses and Monotheism*, Freud extended his analysis of group psychology. But beyond biology and psychology, social dynamics also matter. For instance, William Donald Hamilton, a biologist and social scientist, explored this in *The Genetical Evolution of Social Behaviour*. He proposed the existence of a "social herd instinct" that fosters a collective craziness, shaping people's identities around shared cultural patterns—identical books, foods, fashion, religious practices, or ideological affiliations.

This process often leads individuals to identify with broader social groups—"I am a Muslim, a Sunni, a Shia, an Ahmadi, a Brahmin, a Jew, a Christian, a Pakistani, a Canadian." When viewed through Freud's theories on ego dynamics and dopamine's biological role, we begin to see herd behaviour as an identifiable scientific phenomenon—though certainly not the only explanation.

We must also consider the sociological contributions of Emile Durkheim. His works, *The Division of Labour in Society*, *The Rules of Sociological Method*, *Suicide*, and *The Elementary Forms of Religious Life*, are foundational. He focused particularly on the use of the "sacred"—not just in religious contexts, but secular ones as well. In traditions like Buddhism or Jainism, there is no external deity, yet the systems are considered sacred. Similarly, myths like national anthems and flags are treated with near-religious reverence. Burn a flag, and you'll see the outrage it provokes.

In crowd psychology, collective emotions play a vital role. Manufactured or real feelings of deprivation and injustice can unify a group's ego. The desire to retaliate against perceived oppression, often manifests in aggressive attitudes toward gaining systemic control. During such phases, personal egos dissolve into a tribal group identity. This can escalate into full-blown revolutions or even the creation of nations.

And when, generations later, the enchantment wears off, those born in its wake begin—through rational, critical awareness—to evaluate the gains and losses of it all.

Dr. Muhammad Shahzad:

Doctor Iqbal, when we look around, we see a so-called "religious society." Religion—and its strategic use in politics—has turned us into increasingly self-centered individuals. What role does *herd mentality* play in all of this?

Dr. Baland Iqbal:

Shahzad, I think to understand the use of these two elements—religion and politics—we must first clarify what we mean by *religion*, and then examine how it is employed socially. For instance, a very important question is: what exactly is meant by a *"True Religion"*? In English, we often say, *"True religion is the tool to access your free will."*

So the immediate question becomes: how does *free will* relate to *true religion*? What is the pathway to that connection? Is that path meant to serve *self-interest*, or is it a journey inward—toward the internal metaphysical world of the self? I believe it is the latter.

If so, then does this path pass through a crowd, or does it require solitude—a space apart—for divine reflection and self-realization? Even for basic academic study, we often seek out a library to escape the noise and connect with our books. So how much more solitude would one require when immersing in a divine or spiritual inquiry?

Yes, some people possess such creative capacities that they may occasionally experience inspiration even in a crowd. But for how long? Can you truly build a lasting, intimate connection with the divine while standing or sitting for hours, months, or years amidst a noisy mass of people? Or is it merely a *physical exercise*—reciting verses, perhaps even knowing their meaning, but never diving into their depth—and then saying a quick goodbye to the divine and rushing back out?

I remember my father, a poet and writer, would become so absorbed in his creative work that we children could play around him, and he wouldn't even notice. But when the noise became too much, our mother would quietly signal us to keep it down so he wouldn't be *disturbed*. Spirituality, in this sense, also demands a similar solitude—a space conducive to deep creative and reflective thought. One cannot truly enter the inner journey of *zikr* (divine remembrance) if surrounded by a tumult of loudspeakers, chants, slogans, and instructions blaring into your ears every few seconds.

If we take this seriously, then our *zikr* may become derailed. Consider this: two and a half thousand years ago, when Moses was on Mount Sinai in communion with God, he later addressed a massive crowd. As a prophet, this event can be interpreted from many theological and philosophical angles. But when it comes to an ordinary person gathering a crowd in the name of revelation, we must question whether that gathering is genuinely for the sake of divine inspiration or driven by social or political motives. In fact, we must also assess the ratio between divine and socio-political motivations.

Another vital question: in such a crowded environment, is the religion being invoked really a *True Religion* that leads to free will—or is it a *Political or Social Religion*? Or worse, is it merely an *economic manifestation* of what was once a spiritual doctrine, now shaped by capitalist imperatives?

These kinds of questions not only emerge naturally—they must be asked. We must also critically interrogate the material use of "True Religion" in this context.

And these questions aren't unique to monotheistic religions. They apply just as much to Hinduism, Buddhism, and others. Some might justify it by saying, "People get lost in music too. So why not in divine verses?" But there's a key difference: music is a form of *entertainment*, while sacred thought is a quest for *enlightenment*. If their methods are identical, then religion would be subject to even more intense scrutiny than music.

Now, when it comes to the *social and political* use of religion or any sacred thought, we must closely examine the role of *herd mentality*. How is it operationalized?

Take Nazi Germany: people set the stage for Hitler, a staunch nationalist and racist leader. The sacredness of nationhood and racial superiority was transformed into powerful slogans. Crowds were orchestrated. Specially selected individuals in those crowds led the chants. Hitler skillfully crafted an atmosphere of emotional intensity. He used all of these techniques with calculated precision. He was a master of *herd mobilization*. He understood the mechanics of *coordination* within a crowd.

You'll find these same techniques in nearly every political revolution. But studying them requires an *entirely unbiased* lens. That means you must examine all political, social, and economic movements without falling prey to *herd mentality* yourself. Study them carefully, analytically.

Take the recent example of a massive biological *pandemic* that swept across Asia, Europe, and North America. Do you know that as a result, nearly 5,000 *protests* erupted globally? These fundamentally altered the economic and social landscape of their respective societies and pushed masses of people into a new kind of political and social culture.

Human evolutionary history is filled with such moments of civilizational mobilization. Consider the 19th-century *feminist movement*, which began with struggles for voting and labor rights and culminated in demands for full equality. Or the abolition of slavery, a system that once existed across the world. Or the *Black rights movements*. Or the unholy alliance between the Catholic Church and feudal systems. Or the emergence of secular thought.

In all these cases, *mass consciousness*—herd mentality—was utilized. But the key difference lies in whether it was used positively or negatively. The outcomes, sooner or later, reveal the difference.

Dr. Muhammad Shahzad:

Doctor Iqbal, to what extent do you see the role of herd or mob mentality in the overall social structure of Pakistan?

Dr. Baland Iqbal:

In Pakistan's social fabric, how deeply embedded is the herd mentality? Let's explore this with a couple of examples. Like many other societies, Pakistan and India are no strangers to herd-driven behavior. Think, for instance, of the tragic incident at Abdul Wali Khan University. The university is named after Khan Abdul Wali Khan, the son of Bacha Khan—revered as the "Frontier Gandhi"—a secular Muslim who advocated nonviolence, opposed religious partition, and replaced weapons with pens in the hands of the Pashtuns.

In a university bearing the name of such a progressive figure, a young student, Mashal Khan, was brutally lynched by religious extremists under the pretext of blasphemy. Around twenty to twenty-five students, perhaps joined by others from outside, first beat him and then someone shot him. Initially, investigations stalled, and his father faced immense difficulties. Eventually, public figures like then-Prime Minister Nawaz Sharif and opposition leaders made remarks that, although Mashal Khan was a religious person who offered prayers, he had a "point of view" that he shared on Facebook—implying that his opinion had become his punishment.

During this time, his burial could not even take place in his native village. In stark contrast, another case unfolded: Mumtaz Qadri, who murdered the Governor of Punjab in the name of blasphemy, had more than 200,000 people attend his funeral. So a point of view begins to emerge: Is the entire Pakistani nation trapped in a deep-rooted form of mob mentality?

Once we start this discussion, two schools of thought surface. For instance, liberal thinkers often argue that the blasphemy law, being part of Sharia, is problematic and should be abolished. On the other hand, religious conservatives argue that the formal legal process is too slow—it takes months, even years—and such delays enrage the public, prompting them to take justice into their own hands. Both perspectives carry a hint of truth, but the deeper issue here is the psychology and effects of mob mentality.

After Mashal Khan's case, similar incidents followed: in Sialkot, three individuals killed a mentally ill man over something controversial he had supposedly said thirteen years ago. In another case, someone's car was torched due to a personal vendetta, but the accusation was manipulated to fall under blasphemy.

If such incidents are common in Pakistan, they are equally rampant in India. Consider the case of Pehlu Khan, who was beaten to death over allegations of being a "cow smuggler." Later, a political figure reportedly remarked that there was no need for the public to apologize, as Pehlu Khan had been involved in smuggling "Mother Cow." Here, two distinct events were conflated to normalize a pathological mindset under the guise of cultural or religious defense.

Mob mentality often operates on the belief that "there is power in unity." This collective identity becomes a powerful social club—easy to join with no entry fee. When the time comes, these groups are activated, often by political or religious factions, to eliminate their chosen "villain" under the mask of collective justice. Such groups are often nurtured by the state itself, which helps them evolve for its own ends.

This is where Richard Dawkins' concept of the "meme" or cultural gene becomes relevant—how certain ideas transmit across generations, like genes, and how political and social forces manipulate tribal instincts for their own gain. I believe understanding this entire hierarchy is essential for any conscious individual to avoid descending into the collective madness of mob behavior and to preserve their humanity.

Dr. Muhammad Shahzad:

Sir, we've now understood several critical aspects of herd or mob mentality, and it's clear this is a dangerously potent psychological force. So what, in your view, is the solution?

Dr. Baland Iqbal:

Yes, Shahzad, you're absolutely right—mob mentality is indeed a dangerous phenomenon. We've seen that whether in the East or West, many fascist regimes have relied heavily on it for their rise to power. These regimes often manipulate sacred national or religious slogans to create a specific kind of polarization—and we, the ordinary people, end up bearing the brunt of the consequences.

Interestingly, once fascist states are firmly established, they become quite adept at controlling the very mob mentality they once harnessed. The sources of problems often hold the keys to their own resolution. For instance, in Saudi Arabia or China, strong centralized systems like dictatorships or one-party rule effectively manage mob impulses through force. These countries restrict free speech and expression, tightly control or outright ban social media, and grant its usage only under strict surveillance.

The issue becomes more complex in Western democracies, where values like individualism, human rights, and free expression can sometimes clash with efforts to control mob behavior. However, these societies have also developed legal frameworks that closely monitor the ideologies driving mobs and respond sternly to religious extremism, racism, and inciteful speech.

On an individual level, the most vital remedy is knowledge and awareness. An ordinary person must understand the social and psychological mechanisms behind mob mentality and recognize the dangers it poses. As individuals grow in understanding, they begin to rise above the crowd. They become less susceptible to mass hysteria and start to think independently. In other words, the antidote is education—gained through books or meaningful dialogue.

The more we cultivate knowledge, the more we distance ourselves from the "rush mind" that drives herd behavior. We develop a critical mindset, a personal point of view, different from the masses—one shaped by understanding and reflection. The more objectively we analyze events or ideologies—by considering both sides—we inoculate ourselves against polarization.

Take a simple example: we see a video clip or news item that incites our emotions. It becomes essential to ask: Is this electronic media piece being used as a political or economic tool? We can't blindly trust such reports. But if the same news comes from a credible newspaper like *The Washington Post* or *The New York Times*, we may take it more seriously, knowing that, despite biases, these outlets follow rigorous editorial standards. That kind of scrutiny is absent in the flood of YouTube or TikTok videos.

So the point, Shahzad, is this: just as the Western world managed to separate church and state, we must also learn to distinguish between *opinion* and *fact*. Understanding this difference is crucial. And while we may never completely rid ourselves of mob mentality on an individual level, we can certainly keep a healthy distance from it through awareness, reflection, and critical thinking.

This mind must be kept under the illusion of democracy

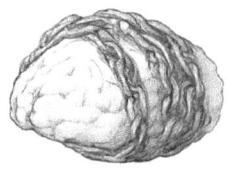

Dr. Muhammad Shahzad:

What is your perspective on democracy? And what are your thoughts on its different forms?

Dr. Baland Iqbal:

Shahzad, whenever we look at world history, we find that most of the governments throughout time were long dominated by dictatorship—whether in the form of *aristocracy*, *tyranny*, *monarchy*, or *totalitarianism*. The common thread among all these systems was that the public had little to no share in governance.

When we talk about democracy, we usually mean a system where the government is genuinely by the people, because the representatives are chosen by the people themselves. If we trace this back to ancient times, we find its roots around 500 BCE with figures like *Cleisthenes*, known as the father of democracy. In the Roman era, democracy was practiced in Athens. The very word "democracy" comes from "demos," meaning people, and "kratos," meaning rule—implying that its foundational idea is people's rule.

In that era, Athens had a formal assembly or council. You may recall that even Socrates' trial was held in a parliamentary setup of about 500 members—220 voted in his favor and 280 against him. He was sentenced to death on the charges of corrupting the youth and questioning traditional religion. The point is, even back then there existed concepts of a parliament and court system, with lawmakers and legal frameworks grounded in democratic procedures.

Moving to the modern era, our attention is drawn first to the *Magna Carta*, signed in England in 1215—also known as the Great Charter. This was the first document to challenge the unchecked authority of the monarchy, essentially telling the king that even he must govern within the boundaries of the *rule of law*. Of course, even after the Magna Carta, monarchy continued in England for centuries because the Catholic Church lent religious legitimacy and support to the monarchy. These two institutions sustained each other's power. It wasn't until the Renaissance—during the 14th and 15th centuries—

that the challenge to church intervention in governance took real shape, though this was far from easy.

Soon after, a wave of political, social, and scientific revolutions and inventions began reshaping the world. Especially the political revolutions brought deep changes. While history often presents these developments in a romantic light, the reality is that this was a bloody and violent period. One of the first major revolutions was the *French Revolution* in 1789. Paradoxically, democracy did not immediately follow this revolution—instead, we saw the rise of the military dictatorship of *Napoleon Bonaparte*. The actual democratic transformation of France only began with the 1848 revolution, which marked the true end of aristocracy and the beginning of a civil democratic structure.

You're right, Shahzad, that democracy didn't emerge right after the 1789 revolution, but a *democratic mindset* was certainly born—primarily because of the people's sacrifices and bloodshed. This gave rise to a powerful ideological shift, a secular consciousness, and the notion of *freedom of speech*.

Turning to the United States, one figure stands out—*Thomas Jefferson*, the third U.S. President. He played a pivotal role in shaping democracy in America by signing the *Declaration of Independence*, a document authored by a council of five. This declaration integrated principles from the Magna Carta into the American Constitution, laying the foundation for religious freedom and secular governance in the U.S. It established that everyone in America would be free to practice their religion—whether in a mosque or church—without any state interference. The separation of church and state naturally led to the rise of civil rights discourse.

Fast-forward about a hundred years to *1864*, and we encounter another towering figure in American democracy—*Abraham Lincoln*. During the time of the Civil War—when tensions between Northern and Southern states over slavery were at their peak—Lincoln delivered a speech containing a phrase that became a textbook definition of democracy:

> "It is the government of the people, by the people, and for the people."

This statement became canon in democratic philosophy. Over the past hundred to hundred and fifty years, democracy has gradually refined and become more established worldwide.

As for the types of democracy, Shahzad, this may sound a bit text bookish, but it's useful to understand. Broadly, democracy can be divided into practical or functional forms.

One was *direct democracy*, where people directly elected their representatives—but this often led to conflict and bloodshed. Later, *indirect democracy* evolved, where groups debated policies and arguments were evaluated before voting. Over time, political parties became central in nominating candidates, and voters began selecting leaders based on party manifestos and the moral or social credibility of the candidates. This remains the dominant form of democracy today: people vote for candidates proposed by political parties. The public may be influenced by the *charismatic* personas of party leaders, their political statements, or party ideology. However, in some more discerning societies, voters choose candidates based solely on party performance—rejecting them in subsequent elections if they underperform.

Textbook-wise, there are two main models:

1. Presidential Democracy, and
2. Parliamentary Democracy—both of which are globally practiced.

From a functional point of view, we also identify constitutional democracies, which are implemented in various countries. For instance, in India, it's called the *Lok Sabha*, currently led by *Narendra Modi*. In Pakistan, we have a parliamentary democracy with a Prime Minister like *Imran Khan*. The UK also follows a parliamentary system, whereas the U.S. practices a presidential model. Interestingly, Britain has retained its traditional monarchy alongside constitutional democracy—though its monarchy today holds more economic and cultural power than political.

Over the past 150 years, a new hybrid has emerged called social democracy, which gives special importance to social issues such as public education, healthcare, housing, basic amenities, pricing of essential goods, human rights, crime prevention, and international trade and political relations. The public increasingly focuses on such issues when voting, basing their electoral decisions on the performance of political parties and candidates on these fronts.

Dr. Muhammad Shahzad:

Alright, sir, those were the fundamentals. Now, please tell us—what challenges does democracy face in establishing itself?

Dr. Baland Iqbal:

Certainly, Shahzad. Let's briefly explore where the real challenges to democracy arise. In some countries, instead of genuine democracy, we witness the rise of an artificial or *pseudo-democracy*. If we look back in history, what did Aristotle say? He pointed to the pervasive system of slavery around him, as he advocated for liberation from mental and social servitude. He spoke of individual freedom. His teacher, Plato, on the other hand, discussed governance in *The Republic*, touching on human nature, but he was fundamentally opposed to traditional democracy. One reason for this was that Socrates' death had been a direct result of a parliamentary vote.

Following Aristotle and Plato's philosophical explorations, we find the emergence of the *Social Contract Theory* during the Renaissance—especially in the political ideologies of Rousseau and John Locke.

The first thing we must ask in any democratic structure is this: Is there true *freedom of assembly*? Can any individual freely join or leave any social or political organization, whether it's a trade union, religious body, or political party? Or do they remain under the control of a party mafia? If control exists, then that institution is not democratic.

Similarly, if a country claims to uphold religious freedom, we must ask: how much freedom is truly granted? Is it just a slogan in a state that is religious in structure, while minorities—Christians, Hindus, Muslims of certain sects like Ahmadis—are persistently harassed? If so, then the claim of democracy is invalid.

Next, how much freedom of expression exists? Are citizens truly free to join the army, bureaucracy, or serve as parliamentary counselors? If these avenues are restricted, then democracy does not exist. We must examine *legal rights*: do minorities receive the same legal protections regardless of race, religion, or ethnicity, and are those protections applied equally and simultaneously? Every component of the democratic framework must be analyzed *one by one* to see whether it aligns with democratic principles. If it doesn't, it's not democracy.

The same goes for *electoral democracy*. Are *civil liberties* being upheld? If not, then again, there is no democracy. After each election cycle, do elected representatives report back to the people on their performance? Do they fulfill the promises they made? If not, then democracy hasn't truly been practiced.

There is an even more dangerous scenario. Sometimes, through electoral systems, political parties are brought to power that are inherently *fascist* in nature. Sometimes, religious fundamentalist parties gain traction by presenting appealing slogans and polished campaigns. In such cases, dictatorship hides behind the mask of democracy—as we saw in Iran. These situations expose a lack of *political maturity* in the public. Democracy itself becomes a subject of disillusionment and critique.

Many fascist parties manipulate *fake information*, exploit *religious and nationalistic slogans*, and feed off people's *emotions*. Through social media, they incite hate, anger, false narratives, and targeted accusations, fostering an environment of extreme polarization—both socially and religiously. This divides the public further, creating a bitter, toxic atmosphere throughout the nation.

True democratic behavior must also be reflected *within* political parties. If leadership is inherited—*hereditary*—and only family members reap the benefits of power, and if internal party elections are non-existent, then such parties are faking democracy. Their internal culture is fundamentally undemocratic.

When political parties operate within the directives of the *establishment*, formulating budgets, projects, and foreign/domestic policies based on *dictation*, it becomes clear that they are a façade. What actually governs is *tyranny*, controlled by a coalition of military generals, judiciary members, and bureaucrats—a deep-rooted establishment. These groups parade political leaders to create an illusion of democracy while monopolizing power.

In such cases, *political engineering* is used to manufacture leaders. They are made popular through artificial slogans and then installed in government—either through manipulated public support or fraudulent votes. This way, blame for public grievances falls on these figureheads, while foreign aid money ends up in the pockets of the establishment.

This entire system points toward a *pseudo-democracy*. The process involves full use of *electronic media*, in coordination with religious institutions, social organizations, and even co-opted *intellectuals*. Journalists are rewarded with land and property. Youth minds are poisoned with sectarian politics and extremist religious ideologies.

In all of this, the *local or national establishment* forges strategic ties with the *international establishment*, turning the entire system into a mafia-like operation. Ordinary people remain unaware of this complex web. They are like lost travelers in a dark wilderness—thinking they are informed, but blindly following their charismatic leaders. In the end, just like the beginning, they remain in darkness—never fully grasping the causes of their personal and national failures. Instead, they spend their lives blaming the opposition for the endless crises they face.

Dr. Muhammad Shahzad:

Dr. Iqbal, what kind of democracy exists in Pakistan, and how is it being practiced?

Dr. Baland Iqbal:

Shahzad, democracy is not being practiced in Pakistan at all. What exists is a fake, superficial form of parliamentary democracy that has been maintained for the past seventy-five years just to show the public—and the world—that such a system is in place. In reality, Pakistan operates under an *oligarchy or aristocracy*.

This ruling group includes top military officers and the politicians they've cultivated. Alongside them are senior judges of the Supreme Court and high-level bureaucrats. Together, they form what is known as the *National Establishment*. This *royal group* runs its own exclusive system of *checks and balances*, monitoring one another internally.

Social or *ethical morality* plays no part in their workings. Public issues are of no real importance—beyond being used for chants in rallies or debates on television. In this structure, the people are often referred to with disdain as *"bloody civilians"*, sometimes even likened to vermin or insects.

This aristocratic class calls itself the *"best qualified citizens"*—the only ones considered suitable to rule. It is this group, and their generations, who have formed Pakistan's ruling class for the past seventy-five years. To secure their position, they have deliberately fragmented the population into linguistic, religious, and ethnic *sects*, preventing any unified resistance from emerging. This has proven to be an extremely effective strategy, delivering near-perfect results.

Perhaps the most critical point, Shahzad, is that this *National Establishment* maintains a direct link with the *International Establishment*. This relationship serves as the *backbone* of Pakistan's fake democratic system.

The international powers are primarily interested in Pakistan's *geopolitical positioning*. What they prefer is not a real democracy, but a *pseudo-democratic regime* that can be easily manipulated via the local establishment. This is precisely why Pakistan was created by the British: to form a Western-aligned barrier against communist nations—a concern they had anticipated even before World War II, especially after the *Soviet Revolution of 1917*.

Later, Pakistan was used as a blockade against communist economic expansion, first through participation in the *Cold War*, and now by hindering regional trade corridors through the narrative of terrorism.

In essence, Pakistan's role in South Asia is similar to that of Israel in the Middle East. Both countries were created on religious foundations to ensure that political stability in these regions remains perpetually elusive. Just as Israel ensures permanent unrest in the Middle East, Pakistan has historically served to counter the geopolitical ambitions of communist or economically rising powers.

This is the reason why genuine democracy has never taken root in Pakistan.

Dr. Muhammad Shahzad:

Since Pakistan is a religious state, do you think democracy can evolve there—or in other religious countries?

Dr. Baland Iqbal:

Shahzad, if we look at all monotheistic religions, we find a common concept of one God—an all-powerful creator of the universe and all living beings, the Alpha and the Omega. His authority is unquestionable. This idea of divine monarchy is echoed consistently in the Torah, the Bible, and the Qur'an. The structural arrangement of these faiths also reflects a hierarchical, monarchist order—there is the sovereign (God), then His messengers or prophets, God's son (in Christian theology), the Holy Spirit, angels, jinn, and various spiritual beings. It is a celestial monarchy with roles similar to a royal court: a king, princes, ministers, courtiers, handmaidens, and servants—all in the service of the divine.

In such a system, naturally, there's no room for a democratic or parliamentary structure—no prime minister, no president, no cabinet of elected officials. There's no concept of a republic. Even in the grandest theological imaginations, God remains a monarch. For example, St. Augustine, writing during the medieval period, authored *The City of God*, not *The Republic of God*. The theological instinct is monarchist by default.

A religious person's faith inherently involves submission to this monarchist system. In Islam, the system is constitutionally embedded through Sharia, which is to be followed with the same—if not greater—compulsory force as belief itself. The same holds true in Catholicism and Judaism, where a similar hierarchy and system of divine reward and punishment in this life and the hereafter exist.

Clearly, in such a governance model, public opinion holds no importance. The will of the people—likes or dislikes—is irrelevant. The system must be accepted as given, and disobedience brings consequences both in this world and the next. In this "Kingdom of God," there is no freedom of speech or critique—something even human monarchies often lack.

Between the 5th and 15th centuries in Europe, an alliance existed between the Catholic Church and monarchy. Charlemagne, for instance, was crowned by Pope Leo III. As the Roman Empire fractured and Germanic and Frankish tribes encroached on the Western Empire, feudalism spread, and the Catholic Church, in collaboration with monarchs (including the Byzantine Empire), began establishing "holy states" and launching the Crusades. These were battles against Islamic states, primarily the Islamic Caliphate.

Whatever the outcome of those wars, they established a clear polarity: Catholic Church vs. Islamic school of governance. In the West, however, things changed. By the Renaissance in the 15th century, the Catholic Church's control crumbled; monarchies and feudalism waned and were replaced by democratic states. Even the Catholic Church itself shrank in power and splintered into various Protestant movements. Unfortunately, no such transformation occurred in the East.

The Ottoman Empire lasted until the 20th century, by which time the concept of the nation-state had already taken root in the West. But the Muslim world saw no similar intellectual awakening. There was no renaissance, no major philosophical or scientific revolution. Politically and socially, things remained stagnant—and the colonization of the East by Western powers only made things worse. The West had no interest in allowing a local intellectual revolution. Instead, they perpetuated monarchist frameworks to maintain control. They profited geopolitically by preserving the alliance between mosque and state.

Pakistan is a product of this very historical backdrop. India at least developed a certain political and social consciousness, but Pakistan was created to serve Western political interests. Hence, the alliance between mosque and a feudalistic state remained intact. That is why secular visions in Pakistan are quickly dismissed as atheistic or un-Islamic. Modernism—essential for scientific and social revolution—has been turned into a slur, branded as Western worship. Consequently, Pakistan was handed over to the equivalent of Europe's Dark Ages.

This is why, even today, the lives of ordinary Pakistanis resemble the devastated masses of Europe between the 5th and 15th centuries—deprived of basic necessities, caught in ethnic, nationalist, and religious extremism, and constantly bleeding from internal conflict. As long as states wear a religious label—whether as "Meccan" or "Medinan" states—these tactics will keep misleading people. Democracy is simply not possible without a secular state. The public must be granted the freedom to form and express opinions. The state must be freed from feudalism so that federal politicians cannot dominate the people. The mosque must be separated from the state so that it may return to its sacred role rather than being exploited politically. Citizens must be provided with basic rights and needs—

but for all of this to happen, there must first be genuine social, political, and religious awareness among the masses.

Dr. Muhammad Shahzad:

Sir, given this deeply troubling situation, is there any *cemented* or *practical* solution?

Dr. Baland Iqbal:

Yes, as I mentioned, this situation is alarming. Over the past 75 years, Pakistan has been ruled by a criminally negligent elite that, in collaboration with the establishment, has created zombie-like statues—citizens who see intellect and critical thinking as enemies. These are people afflicted with herd and mob mentality. They consider Western political thought and philosophical traditions to be hostile.

But the West's political maneuvering and its intellectual tradition are not the same. Their political actions may at times be against us, but it is their philosophical and scientific advancements that have made them powerful. They separated the Church from the state and established secular governments. Their modern state model led them to global dominance. They were once on the same path of decay that we are on now—but they realized it was a road to destruction and turned away from it. We too must approach these issues *non-biasedly*.

I believe we should intellectually revisit 399 BCE and examine what happened to Socrates. True, he suffered under democracy, but he did not become an enemy of it. He believed democracy had the potential for civilizational progress—*if* it were true democracy, not one engineered by local or international establishments. Plato later turned against democracy, believing that once it is hijacked by dominating powers, it turns into tyranny—a form of rule even worse than monarchy. Pakistan is experiencing just such tyranny today.

Socrates offered a solution through *rationality*. He believed in educating people politically and socially, in open criticism of institutions, in judging leaders based on performance rather than charisma, and in preventing religious ideology from hijacking state institutions. And if that is not possible, then societies must explore *alternate experiments*.

It is entirely plausible that different nations have different social and economic realities. Not all citizens are politically educated enough to vote responsibly. In societies where people are easily swayed by mob emotions, where religious manipulation is rampant, where clerics and feudal politicians exploit public sentiment for power, then giving everyone equal voting rights becomes almost absurd.

Singapore tried an experiment in *technocracy*. There, technocrats contested elections and led the country toward positive change. These professionals are practical-minded, not ideologically rigid. With a fair system of checks and balances, such experiments are worth considering. It worked in Singapore.

Voting rights could be tied to education. Citizens' political and social understanding could be tested—because not everyone is automatically entitled to a vote. This is undoubtedly controversial, but it deserves discussion. All of this, however, is only possible with freedom of expression.

Pakistan's intellectuals must step forward. It is their *intellectual responsibility* to educate the public, otherwise their presence and popularity mean nothing while the nation plunges into ruin.

Simone de Beauvoir, the French feminist and philosopher, once harshly criticized French intellectuals for their silence when German forces entered Paris during World War II. She called this behavior *disinterested contemplation*—a selfish detachment driven by concern for personal image rather than national crisis. The Italian post-Marxist revolutionaries called such writers "non-organic intellectuals"—their presence or absence makes no difference.

Pakistan is currently overrun with such writers and political commentators. Either they remain silent or resort to shallow commentary for fame and wealth. Sadly, the people of Pakistan suffer the most from this, because it means they are denied the very political and social consciousness they so desperately need.

This mind must be trapped in a tribal patriarchal mentality

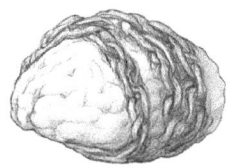

Dr. Muhammad Shahzad:

Dr. Iqbal, whenever we think about our society, it feels distinctly different from typical societies around the world. Here, many unusual issues exist that we often tend to conceal. There are numerous problems which we, while considering them real, continuously try to justify by attaching various ideological justifications. For example, the patriarchal system we have here—called *Narwaki Nizam* in Pashto, meaning "male dominance"—is a cancerous power spread throughout society. Doctor, today's topic is exactly this. My first question for you in this regard is: historically, where do the roots of this male dominance system come from?

Dr. Baland Iqbal:

Certainly, Shahzad. The patriarchal system refers to the dominance or supremacy of men in society. Since we are talking about men here, it specifically refers to a sexual patriarchy—that is, a society where being male is considered a privilege. As a result, men gain a free social advantage and obtain the right to dominate women, control them, or exploit them. Such a system is known as patriarchy.

The word "patriarchal" itself is derived from two Greek words: "patriarch" meaning "father" or "man," and "archē" meaning "authority." So, it literally means "men's control" or "men's monopoly on authority." Let's take a brief historical glance at this entire system.

Shahzad, you know that when we study human civilization's overall history, we generally divide it into two parts: the Stone Age and the Iron Age. This means roughly six thousand years ago—four thousand years before the birth of Jesus Christ—human history is classified as the Stone Age, during which there was no formal writing system, so few social facts can be traced. But as time progressed, entering the Copper and then the Bronze Age, many historical evidences started to emerge.

We are talking about a period about 1,000 to 1,500 years before the birth of Christ, when established Bronze Age societies existed. This dates back roughly four thousand years, when humans passed through the agricultural revolution, started forming small, organized settlements like villages, and the concept of the state began to emerge. Mythical stories gave rise to various religious beliefs flourishing in society, which were being organized by religious scholars. Places of worship became institutions, and rules and laws for customs and traditions were being formulated. Writing was discovered, languages developed, and knowledge became a fundamental part of society's fabric.

Mathematics, astronomy, and philosophy became part of human intellectual development. Human consciousness was advancing day by day. During this period, all civilizations—whether Indian, Chinese, or especially those in the Middle East, which we might call the Ancient East—developed under organized governments. These included regions like Persia (northwest Iran), Anatolia in Turkey, Azerbaijan, Israel, Palestine, and areas of modern Syria and Iraq.

In all these civilizations, roughly four to five thousand years ago, a patriarchal system was found. Shahzad, there are many books and references on this subject. For example, you may recall Friedrich Engels, who, alongside Karl Marx, wrote the famous book *The Origin of Family, Private Property, and the State*. They linked the entire patriarchal system with class division. They argued that men gave their property only to male children, while women's role was to bear children and manage the household. Men were responsible for the economic sustenance of the family.

However, an American historian, Gerda Lerner, in her book *The Creation of Patriarchy*, challenged this historical conception. She argued that patriarchy was established even before class divisions emerged. She traced this back to Aristotle, who believed women were morally, mentally, and physically inferior to men and considered women as men's property. Aristotle thought women's purpose was only to bear children and serve men. According to him, men are naturally dominant in society, a superior gender compared to women, who he saw as incomplete and incapable of producing perfection. He declared patriarchy as natural and ordained by nature.

Obviously, once such theories become established, they perpetuate from generation to generation. Children grow up observing this mindset in their families, accept it as natural, and eventually these customs become ingrained in their very blood or genes. If we study later Greek and Egyptian societies, we find Athens was quite different from Egypt. Athens was far more patriarchal than Egypt. Interestingly, two to two and a half millennia before Christ, Egyptian women had more rights than their Greek counterparts. Middle-class Egyptian women worked alongside men outside the home; they were involved in property, business, and real estate, signed documents, and managed commercial affairs. They were socially active, whereas Athens lagged behind in these regards. Women in Athens had few rights and the society was dominated by men. Given Aristotle's patriarchal views and his student Alexander the Great ruling Greece, it's no surprise the entire society moved forward along these lines.

Similarly, in China during that era, Confucius taught patriarchal principles. His book *The Three Obediences and Four Virtues* assigned women a subordinate status. According to Confucius, before marriage a woman must obey her father, after marriage her husband, and if widowed, her eldest son. Women were expected to remain loyal to men because they were considered male sexual property. In short, human society has remained patriarchal since ancient times.

Dr. Muhammad Shahzad:

Doctor Iqbal, is the patriarchal system hereditary by nature, or is it an artificial system created by men solely to rule over women?

Dr. Baland Iqbal:

Shahzad, this is a very interesting question: is patriarchy truly hereditary, or is it an artificial system disguised as natural? Social scientists mostly argue that it is entirely artificial. Genetically, men are not programmed to control women. Rather, this is a result of cultural and evolutionary stages where men seek to control women socially.

This aligns with the feminist movement's perspective—that patriarchy is an artificial social behavior rooted in tribal mentality and must now change. Two fundamental questions arise from feminism: why do men want to control women, and how do they use power against women? They argue that this system has a purely social and historical basis. If it were natural, how could it be natural? Traditionally, tribal-minded people believe these are religious commands, and since religion is a natural process for them, this is a divine command, completely natural and unquestionable.

They claim that nature created men with distinct physical attributes—larger size, stronger bones and muscles, and even bigger brains. But this raises the question: does a bigger brain mean higher intelligence? When we examine psychological and cognitive scales of men and women, we find many contradictions. Intelligence should be measured not by size but by memory, reasoning power, aggression, and patience.

For instance, men have one X and one Y chromosome, while women have two X chromosomes. Genetically, it's proven that X chromosomes carry much more information than Y chromosomes. Richard Lippa's book *Gender, Nature, and Nurture* discusses social differences between men and women in detail. According to him, men and women show moderate differences in social and emotional status.

In work preferences, men generally like to work with things or machines, while women prefer working with people. Men are typically "things-oriented," women "people-oriented." Another interesting fact is that men are more disturbed by a woman's physical or sexual infidelity, whereas women suffer more from a man's emotional infidelity. A study at the University of Wisconsin developed around 25 psychological, cognitive, and communication variables and applied them to social dynamics but found no significant performance differences between men and women.

Their conclusion: if women are given equal opportunities, they perform just as well as men. The only difference lies in preferences: women prefer working in social environments like schools, nursing homes, and hospitals where interaction is high, while men prefer mechanical environments.

In summary, men and women have equal intelligence, and patriarchy is merely an artificial system.

Dr. Muhammad Shahzad:

Doctor Iqbal, then who is responsible for this patriarchal system? Did it come into existence solely because of men, or are women equally to blame for its establishment?

Dr. Baland Iqbal:

Shahzad, that is indeed a very interesting question: is the patriarchal system the responsibility of men alone, or have women also played a role behind it? In my view, a clap never comes from just one hand, and similarly, this issue is not one-sided. Over centuries, the patriarchal system has become part of women's psychology, and whether consciously or unconsciously, women have also been involved in supporting and sustaining it.

In the last two to three hundred years, serious struggles against patriarchy have mainly occurred in the West. We have notable figures such as Elizabeth Stanton, who wrote *The Woman's Bible*; Betty Friedan, author of *The Feminine Mystique*; Simone de Beauvoir, whose long feminist struggle and famous bestseller *The Second Sex* are well known; and Emma Goldman, who fought extensively for anarchism.

Similarly, in Pakistan, significant work has been done on this subject. We have feminist writers like Fahmida Riaz and Kishwar Naheed, as well as social activists like Asma Jahangir and Malala Yousafzai, who have worked for women's rights across various fields and spoken out boldly against male dominance. However, the problem is that in Pakistan and many other Islamic countries, the patriarchal system is actively supported at the governmental level—the state deliberately seeks to uphold and perpetuate this entire system.

As for women themselves, it is somewhat true that alongside men, women have also tried to maintain this patriarchal society. Ninety percent of Pakistani women have fallen prey to patriarchal psychology; their temperament is thoroughly religious, and they regard male authority over themselves as divine command. This psychology runs so deep that they actually *enjoy* this dependency, become addicted to it, and even take advantage of it.

Interestingly, women who are not religious seem affected by patriarchy in somewhat different ways. For example, if you talk to women anywhere in the world on this topic, you will encounter a different mindset. Even in the West, we get some intriguing responses from women, such as: "Oh, dominating men are like oxygen," or "Children of dominating men tend to be very successful," or "Dominating men are very forceful," or "We like to follow dominating men," or "There is a sense of security behind dominating men."

Look at the body language of these dominating men—the charisma of their personalities, the way they walk, talk, and their confidence. Some women even go as far as openly saying that dominating men sexually awaken them.

Now, if such mindsets or psychologies become established in societies, it is clear that the roots of patriarchal society will spread and grow deep in both men and women, like a thick tree, making reform or remedy almost impossible.

Dr. Muhammad Shahzad:

Dr. Iqbal, can we then say that religion has played the backbone role in the patriarchal system?

Dr. Baland Iqbal:

Absolutely, there is no doubt that religion acts as the backbone of the patriarchal system. We find patriarchy particularly in societies where tribal-era beliefs, customs, and laws are still practiced. Especially in societies founded on religious ideologies, patriarchal systems prevail.

If we talk about monotheistic religions, the very word for God is 'He'—a masculine usage—even though God tells us not to view Him as male or female. Moreover, all the prophets who came were men; there is no mention of any female prophet or daughter of God.

Look at worship practices: women do not lead prayers. Consider the story of Adam and Eve—God created Adam with His own hands, but when it came to Eve, she was created from Adam's ribs. One wonders why God did not create Eve the same way He created Adam. Was it to give her a lower status? Likewise, when Adam was expelled from Paradise, the blame fell on Eve's temptation.

In Christianity, Mary is called the Virgin Mary—why was Mary's virginity necessary for Jesus's birth? Are all women who give birth not pure? Is childbirth considered an impure act?

It does not end there—religion even permits men to physically discipline their wives, yet women are not allowed to "disrespect" their husbands no matter how sinful or cruel they may be. After God, the husband holds the highest status, and women are commanded to cover themselves like sexual objects to prevent men's "indecency." Why is it that men's nature is so easily aroused?

Women's worship is also prescribed primarily at home, which supposedly grants more reward. In wartime, women are expected to serve men or pray at home. In Paradise, men are promised the finest houris (virgins), but there is no promise of good men for virtuous women. If a woman is pious, she will get her old husband again in Heaven. Men, however, can marry up to four wives even in the afterlife; women do not get that privilege.

Similar patterns exist in other religions. For example, Hinduism prescribes that a widow should immolate herself on her husband's funeral pyre (sati), but there is no religious injunction for the husband to do anything if the wife dies. Even in the Buddha era, if you search remote villages in the Himalayas, you might find a female ascetic, but the Buddhist branch prescribes that no matter how virtuous a woman is, she cannot reach Nirvana unless she is reborn as a man first.

The irony is that in such religious societies, women themselves take pride in placing themselves in a subordinate position—they feel a sense of pride or are very proud of this status. When conditions are this dire, one tends to believe Aristotle's statement that women really do have some intellectual issues along with their gender.

Dr. Muhammad Shahzad:

Dr. Iqbal, has Western society found any solution to the patriarchal system or this sick mentality? Because here, the common perception is that patriarchy does not exist in the West, but there, women have become completely disrespected and dishonored. What is your opinion on this?

Dr. Baland Iqbal:

Look, Shahzad, I have been living in Western countries for the past twenty to twenty-two years, and my experiences are quite different. Let me put it simply: every year, thousands of families move here from the Middle East to the US and Canada. Can you find even one family whose women want to go back to the Middle East? Men may face various problems, especially related to jobs, but women thoroughly enjoy this society. Here, they find a society that is highly matriarchal. They quickly realize that this society favors women greatly. In fact, women's rights here are genuinely much stronger than men's—whether it's reproductive rights, family laws, job-related matters, or domestic violence issues.

For example, if you stare at a woman walking down the street or in a market in these countries, it could lead to a harassment case. Our society, however, is full of such incidents with no accountability. Look at the conditions in our offices, markets, streets, schools, and colleges — they are known to all of us. Videos of such cases surface regularly. But here, such incidents are often hidden due to fear of disgrace. Another excuse given is that reporting such cases would dishonor our country or religion. However, in the West, there is no such baseless fear of dishonor. If a wrong has been done legally, it is wrong, and the perpetrator is punished. The laws here are extremely strict and largely fair. That is why no woman on the street is shouted at; no one snatches purses or earrings from women. Women, regardless of their attire, are generally not even glanced at.

When it comes to legal crimes, they can happen anywhere, but the West has taken very stringent legal action against them. There has been serious work done to uphold women's rights here, such as voting rights and labor rights. Men and women receive equal pay, and educational disparities between genders have been eliminated. I remember when I went to Dow Medical College, there were fewer admission seats for girls than boys because it was argued that women generally leave their seats during studies due to marriage, etc., and often do not complete their degrees. But in reality, that is not true. Women are working in medical research, technical jobs, computer fields, and health institutions. They join these institutions at every stage of life.

No matter what misconceptions some may spread, the truth is that this is a society of equality—though men and women may have different responsibilities. In the West, you won't see a scenario where a woman has to work under men merely because she is a woman. Women often become CEOs or heads of large companies, and many men work under them. Women have also entered parliament and become ministers. True, in our countries too, women have become prime ministers, but the credit for all this transformation belongs entirely to the West. This change has come about due to serious efforts by women over the past two decades, benefiting women worldwide.

This entire transformation was possible due to the breaking of the patriarchal system in the West, largely because of the collapse of the Catholic system there. Instead of a patriarchal system, a society with equal rights for men and women was established. Interestingly, in our region, many deliberate efforts have been made to block this positive change. Numerous negative narratives about Western society have been spread—such as claims that the family system there broke down, religion disappeared, immorality spread, children became homeless, elders were neglected in old age homes, and so on.

But if we analyze dispassionately the state of Pakistan, India, or any other developing Eastern society, where are these problems greater? Look at the condition of family systems in Pakistan: people do "social marriages" for show, women suffer abuse from husbands, mothers-in-law, sisters-in-law, often leading to murder or being burnt alive. Gas cylinders don't explode on their own in kitchens. The stress and anxiety women endure in forced loveless marriages and their in-laws' houses are sky-high. Tragically, family members kill each other over small sums of money, refuse to care for their parents, shift responsibilities, hurl accusations, and the elderly and young alike endure harshness and disrespect.

Women incessantly criticize their husbands' families, and men mock their wives' families. Are these the signs of a civilized society? No. These are signs of a hypocritical, artificial society where people do not speak the truth, live by false traditions, suffer psychological problems, talk about religion, pray, perform Hajj, fill mosques, and selfishly strive for paradise, but have no real compassion or empathy for their families or elders. They wrap themselves in the blanket of religion, consider the afterlife as the true life, and live in a permanent delusion or misunderstanding, remaining in a comfort zone and going through their days like that—wasting their entire lives.

The result is that serious discussion on real issues never happens, nor is there any attempt to establish a plan for the future generations or even their own old age. Thus, each new generation suffers the same problems as the previous one, deceiving themselves like their elders, and live a life full of pain and torment.

The reality that the West understood long ago was hinted at much earlier by Karl Marx, who said that the capitalist system would destroy family values, customs, and traditional notions of family and marriage. Therefore, capitalism's solution was nursing homes and old age houses. Now, this is happening worldwide, and these problems have somewhat been alleviated. Many nursing homes here are free from the domestic abuse and quarrels common in homes in India and Pakistan.

It is true that in capitalist societies marriages began to be formed more on professional and social status bases rather than love, and eventually these marriages also started breaking down—though such bad conditions were not present in the 18th and 19th centuries, when a balance between family, religion, customs, and traditions was maintained. But as societies became more mechanical, family systems deteriorated, and this also happened in Eastern societies where capitalism's effects were even more severe.

Another point is that here, Western society is often introduced to us through immoral films, just as Western media portrays the slums and customs of India, Pakistan, or the Middle East as backward. Clearly, this is done to uphold the capitalist system and gain political advantages. But just as Pakistan's society is not merely the streets of Heera Mandi (Red Light District), similarly the West is not just nightclubs. Many families live here in very traditional ways, with values upheld, much like honorable families in Pakistan and India.

It is true that both the West and the East have their problems—some greater, some lesser—but the solution lies in an open mind, impartial thinking, and political awareness, because that is what human civilization demands for improvement.

This mind must be fed lies about secularism.

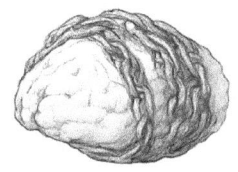

Dr. Muhammad Shahzad:

Sir, there are many concerns about the issue of secularism in general and especially within Pakistani society, which need to be discussed. My first question is: What is your view on secularism from a historical and geographical perspective?

Dr. Baland Iqbal:

Yes, Shahzad, let us talk a little about secularism today. Friends, secularism is often portrayed very negatively among the general public in Pakistan, deliberately twisted to mislead people against Western thought. The masses here have been led to believe that secularism means disbelief or atheism, and it has been forcefully fed to them as such. Poor people get nightmares even just googling the term. This intellectual dishonesty has been perpetrated mainly by religious institutions, who, as scholars, ought to uphold intellectual honesty, at least be accountable to their own conscience. After all, ethics and morality have been their domain through religion, and they have enjoyed the highest social status as the bearers of virtue and goodness. Obviously, there are political motives behind this deception which remain hidden from the public eye.

Is there really any connection between secularism and atheism? Is there a genuine philosophical or psychological reason, or is this merely the insecurity of religious institutions fearing that if secularism is established, their sinister plans to maintain power will be thwarted, and power will shift to ordinary people?

Let us first honestly look at the textbook definition of secularism. According to standard texts, a secular state is one where:

"The political affairs of a state are kept separate from its religious affairs."

In any state, the religious matters of the people should not be entangled in political affairs or controlled by political institutions. People should be allowed to live their lives according to their beliefs. A state hosts people of various religions who have the full right to live peacefully within it. They should have the freedom to worship in their places of worship—whether temples, churches, mosques, synagogues, shrines, or dargahs—in their own ways and find mental peace.

To understand this concept's background, we need to turn back a few pages of history. Let's see what the situation was like in Greek states two thousand years before Christ. Were they secular or democratic? Yes, they were limitedly democratic, but not secular. Evidence of this is the patriarchal society there, divided into aristocrats and slaves. Although there was a senate and councils, women and slaves were not allowed to vote. The lack of secularism is evident in the fate of Socrates, who was sentenced to death by hemlock because he was accused of openly challenging traditional religions and misleading the youth. This shows that society then was non-secular and only limitedly democratic, where even freedom of expression was restricted.

Now, let's briefly come to the medieval period, after the era of Socrates and Aristotle, following the collapse of powerful Greek city-states. In Europe, between the 5th and 15th centuries, democracy was nowhere to be seen. Instead, aristocracy, monarchy, and dictatorship prevailed. Similarly, in the East, during the establishment of Muslim states like the Rashidun and Abbasid Caliphates—often called the golden age of Islam—monarchies dominated. The Caliphs ruled as hereditary kings, and there was no experience of democracy similar to the Roman Empire. Was there secularism in these states? The answer is mixed. In some Abbasid monarchies, Jewish scholars worked alongside Muslims, and treatment of minorities was comparatively lenient, especially compared to the Catholic Church.

Now, if we look at Europe after the 15th century, the age of Enlightenment brought modern thinking and started separating the church and the ruling class. The Thirty Years' War and plagues had devastated Europe, weakening the Catholic Church and state institutions. Scientific and philosophical revolutions by Newton, Copernicus, Galileo, and philosophers like Francis Bacon, Thomas Hobbes, John Locke, Voltaire, Hegel, and Immanuel Kant challenged old orthodoxies. The Protestant Reformation led by Martin Luther King and Rousseau's social contract theory, alongside economic ruin from wars and pandemics, paved the way for the French, British, and American revolutions. Monarchism and religious states crumbled, and a new human society was built on secularism—the principle that state institutions cannot monopolize or control people's beliefs—because such control was the root cause of destruction in the East and West.

Thus, from a geographical perspective, Europe provides us with a full picture. If we turn to North America, there is a rich history of secular thought, especially after America freed itself from British colonization. Figures like Thomas Jefferson and James Madison were pioneers in trying to incorporate secularism into the American constitution. This phase between 1801 and 1817 is significant, as secularism began to be practiced in earnest only after the 20th century.

Earlier, the situation was different. Although the 19th century marked the beginning, actual implementation is evident around 1860–1870. In Britain, the scholar George Jacob Holyoake is credited with introducing the term secularism in 1891. In Turkey, Mustafa Kemal Atatürk officially declared and modernized secularism in 1923. Egypt followed, and in India, secularism came via Gandhi. Finally, your Pakistan came into the picture, where, as you know, this political philosophy led to a great deal of upheaval.

Dr. Muhammad Shahzad:

Sir, when the issue of secularism in Pakistani society was handed over to political powers by the state authorities, what benefits did the political powers gain from it, and what losses did the public or the state itself suffer?

Dr. Baland Iqbal:

Why was secularism in Pakistan deliberately handed over to political conflicts? What advantages did the Pakistani state powers derive from this, and what harm did the people suffer? It is essential to understand all these issues impartially. For a moment, we must recall the foundational ideology proposed for Pakistan — the Two-Nation Theory — and also remember Muhammad Ali Jinnah's 1938 speech made before Pakistan's creation, which was criticized for involving religion in politics. In his defense, Jinnah said that the flag of the Muslim League was not just a political flag, but also the flag of Islam. He expressed pride in his association with Islam, which is not merely a religious doctrine but also a philosophy, politics, and law.

Similarly, in 1945, addressing students at a gathering in the North-West Frontier Province, he declared that the construction of Pakistan was not just a freedom movement but a Muslim ideology. In 1948, speaking at the Karachi Bar Association, he remarked on the confusion people had about Pakistan's constitution not implementing Sharia law, stating that Islamic principles were as effective practically today as they were 1,400 years ago.

However, in his famous August 11 speech, which is often cited to argue that Jinnah wanted a secular state, he addressed minorities in clear terms, assuring them complete freedom to worship in their own temples, mosques, or churches:

"You are free; you are free to go to your temples. You are free to go to your mosques or to any other places of worship in this State of Pakistan. You may belong to any religion, caste or creed—that has nothing to do with the business of the state."

— Muhammad Ali Jinnah

Later, in February 1948, while addressing people in the USA, he explicitly said that Pakistan was not to be a religious state; it had no "priest or divine mission." Muslims, Hindus, Christians, and Parsis all lived in Pakistan and would equally enjoy the right to live there and participate fully in its affairs and development.

Viewed through these speeches, we see both the presence of Sharia laws and Islamic ideology alongside the idea of a secular state. Jinnah appeared to accept the concept of secularism within Islam and sought to build Pakistan accordingly — not on the basis of Western secular thought, but tailored to Islamic understanding.

If we momentarily set aside political diplomacy and defend these statements, they make positive sense. Yet, there is a question about other states: do Hinduism or Christianity inherently embrace secularism? Is that why those states cling to Western secular concepts? Do those states deny people of other faiths the right to practice their religions?

The problem lies in human society, not divine or superhuman values, which every religion possesses in abundance. The corruption of the Catholic Church led to the emergence of secular concepts focused on ordinary society.

Let us glance at India's history: during pre-colonial times under Ghori and Mughal rule, Islam was considered protective of minorities, and Hindus were the majority. But once Gandhi's India emerged, Muslims felt threatened, and the demand for a state in the name of Islam became necessary to safeguard Muslim rights. From 1947 to 1955, Pakistan was introduced internationally as a secular state because the constitution had not yet been formed. But in 1956, when the constitution was promulgated, martial law also came into effect. Pakistan became the Islamic Republic of Pakistan, and by 1977 Sharia law was introduced. Jinnah's Republic thus transformed into General Zia-ul-Haq's Islamic Sharia Republic.

You may ask, what difference did this make compared to India? You are right: a similar spectacle unfolded there as well. India declared itself a secular state for 66 years until Narendra Modi's arrival in 2014 transformed secular India into a Hindu nationalist state inspired by Vinayak Damodar Savarkar.

If Pakistan changed in 1977 with the rise of Muslim clerical culture—beards, cloaks, veils, and scarves—then India changed in 2014 with the prominence of Hindu dhoti and tilak.

So the question remains: is the problem in religious philosophy, which can never be truly secular? These are mere assertions or divine claims. Or is it rather corruption, the same one adopted by the Catholic Church, whereby religion is used as a cover to seize control of government institutions?

Therefore, secular ideology must be included distinctly and strictly in the constitution through laws to ensure its actual implementation. Instead of theoretical debates, practical laws are essential—laws that prevent any political party from exploiting people's faith and emotions to gain vote power.

In a multicultural, multi-linguistic, multi-religious, and multi-economic country like Pakistan, political parties enjoy enormous advantages to easily manipulate a divided nation. In addition, the feudal system, public ignorance, emotionalism, political illiteracy, and unconsciousness are factors that national and international powers exploit with great ease.

Examples abound in Pakistan's history of how the dominating powers have taken advantage of the public. The experiment of Basic Democracy is unparalleled anywhere else in history. There may be no other country where we see the farce of civilian martial law, such as when civilian Zulfikar Ali Bhutto imposed martial law, or General Musharraf ruled as a civilian CEO of the state.

Recently, during Imran Khan's government, despite being a parliamentary leader, he refused to attend parliament sessions, deeming dialogue an insult. He ran parliament from the Prime Minister's House, formed NAB-like organizations, and imprisoned opponents while calling them corrupt, thus bringing disgrace to the country.

The head of NAB, who prosecutes cases on morality, was himself embroiled in sexual scandals. Inside, there was deceit, blackmail, and political maneuvering. When we remember August 11, when Jinnah hinted at a secular state, doesn't it seem that since then, deliberately, the country has been steered in a particular direction to seize power?

In the last 75 years, haven't Ahmadis, Shias, and other religious minorities been persecuted? Didn't Taiseer Sahib get killed? Didn't the crowds at the funerals of his killer and the victim differ? Doesn't that show who the Pakistani public sympathizes with? Or that they hold an anti-secular mindset?

Is blasphemy law not included in the constitution? Were the Hudood Ordinances not incorporated into law? Why did extremist ideology spread during Zia-ul-Haq's era?

Look, the problem is this: the civilian politicians, bureaucracy, madrassas, and military heads shape foreign and domestic policies. The slogan of enmity with India is the best tool. The century-old Kashmir dispute is a lucrative business investment. Border skirmishes in Afghanistan are a thriving enterprise that draws huge geopolitical dollars from nations.

If secularism came to Pakistan, all these practical tools for extracting dollars would slip from the hands of the dominating powers. So who would voluntarily destroy their own interests?

Hence, through media and other commercial institutions influential among the public, secularism is labeled a curse, branded atheism or modernism, and tagged as an enemy of Islam and religion. This narrative is repeated so often that, like Hitler's lie, it is accepted as truth. People never study this ideology objectively, and those who support it are considered "hardcore infidels."

You might recall the "hegemony theory" by Antonio Gramsci. Since Pakistan's inception, secularism has been consistently assigned to controversy and exploited politically to manipulate the public.

Dr. Muhammad Shahzad:

Sir, how can secularism harm religious narratives? Or may I put it this way: Could you shed light on what effects the spread of secularism might have on the interests of the state or state powers?

Dr. Baland Iqbal:

Yes, Shahzad. The spread of secular ideas threatens to wrest power from religious state authorities, as happened in Europe during the era of the Catholic Church. You have observed that once the notion of separation between state and religion began to take root, and a legal separation was established, the religious state's grip on power gradually loosened.

But the question remains: does such a political process actually harm religion? In reality, the religious mindset tends to view this entire secular concept as a whole, understanding it as a theory emerging from Europe's revolutionary intellectual movements of the fifth century—what they call the Renaissance. In Muslim countries, the Muslim mind confronts or interprets this through an Islamic perspective or lens. Meanwhile, traditional Christian and Jewish minds embraced this new intellectual revolution by separating it from religious thought, treating it as a distinct scientific worldview.

This was perhaps because both sides were present—meaning, Jewish and Christian philosophers and scientists stood alongside religious scholars during this new intellectual awakening, so no natural paranoia developed. However, Muslim circumstances were different. Since Muslims had little contribution in philosophy and science at the time, state and religious powers labeled secular thought as anti-religious and easily exploited it to their advantage.

In Europe, during the Renaissance and the rise of modernism, the scientific experiments and observations of Copernicus, Galileo, and Newton gradually posed challenges to religious beliefs. When philosophers like René Descartes declared skepticism the foundation of knowledge—placing doubt against faith—the fundamental tenet of blind belief was severely undermined, and cracks began to appear in the religious conceptual framework.

Similarly, when we discuss the ideas of John Locke, George Berkeley, and David Hume—such as individual freedom of thought and expression, or the state's legal responsibility to protect the life, property, betterment, and peaceful development of its people—these rights often conflict directly or indirectly with the divine or "City of God" concepts held by clerical authorities, who believe all rights belong solely to God, the ultimate sovereign.

Science, being empirical and relying on natural laws, is also seen as controlled by God or nature. The social contract theory of Locke and Rousseau directly clashes with religious thought.

There is also historical context to consider. After the French Revolution, when Napoleon Bonaparte invaded Egypt, he brought printing presses, machines, and dozens of scientists with him to introduce Western ideas, much like other dominant powers, as a formula to spread Western thought in the East. This created paranoia in religious minds that secularism was not just irreligious but a political weapon of Western powers designed to undermine Eastern civilization and impose Western cultural norms—shifting sovereignty from God to the individual.

Thus, if one thinks carefully, secularism was portrayed as a threat to religious thought. But rather than accept this paranoia, one should realize that if secularism truly harmed religion, Christianity and Judaism would have long since disappeared in the West. On the contrary, Christianity remains the largest religion worldwide. Western intellectuals understood the cultural value of religion and would not have so easily discarded it from their societies.

In other words, political conflicts aside, philosophical and scientific wisdom and its benefits stand apart. People living in the East should understand that there is no shame in adopting good and positive ideas to improve their lives, just like ordinary Christians have done.

Dr. Muhammad Shahzad:

Doctor Iqbal, there is a common popular notion among our people that if secularism arrives, we will become Westernized, our morals will deteriorate, our new generation will become rebellious, or Pakistan will drift towards irreligion. Sir, do you think these associations made with secularism are mere assumptions, or are they true?

Dr. Baland Iqbal:

All this is pure propaganda. Secularism neither harms religion nor Eastern traditions. However, it certainly threatens dominant powers because they lose their position to control the masses by collaborating with religious forces. To understand this, we must look at history.

We have lived in the West for the last thirty years—what harm has come to us or our children? Our religious culture remains with us, our Eastern traditions are still practiced, often even better. We have become more truthful and sincere, not less. Our new generation growing up here is morally sound.

No, Shahzad, none of this has any connection to secularism. Religious people in our society often use derogatory slang like "Westernized" to describe this, equating it with obscenity, moral decay, or ruin—warning that secularism will spread such things in society. This paranoia or opposing notion is spread for political reasons, to keep the public confused and under control through religious institutions. It also involves nepotism and sectarian politics, keeping people entangled in hatred and violence while the ruling class continues to govern.

In reality, secularism is an honest social concept meaning simply that in any society where rich, poor, and middle-class people live together, people of different religions also coexist and have equal rights. Everyone has the freedom to worship peacefully in their temples, mosques, churches, etc. In a balanced and just society, subjects are equal—whether rich or poor, Muslim or Hindu, Sunni or Shia, educated or illiterate—everyone should have equal opportunities because they are all equal in the eyes of God.

If they are good or bad, reward or punishment is determined either by the country's law or by God after death. No other human has the right to oppress someone simply because they belong to a different tribe or sect. Such behavior is outright sinful in the eyes of God and the law. This system of justice is called secularism, and it is disliked by rulers who came to power through illegitimate means and deceive the public with false religious narratives, spreading hatred through hired clerics.

Similarly, these rulers generate misplaced fears about modernism, associating the word "modern" with obscenity or Westernization, although modernism was a major intellectual and political movement involving decades of wars in the West and the establishment of a modern scientific society aimed at improving ordinary human lives—something entirely absent in religious societies like ours in Pakistan today.

Many rulers deliberately keep people away from the modern scientific world, spreading misunderstandings about Western civilization to exploit their rights. However, once people from religious societies visit the West, they witness a beautiful life and rarely want to return, realizing how their rulers have wronged them. Those who sincerely try to convey these ideas to their new generation are called rebels, although they are simply exposing political corruption honestly.

So, where is the rebellion in that? Even if it is rebellion, it is a very pure and necessary one.

If we want to view modernization from a fresh perspective, we must look back at history, such as what happened with Turkey. Until the 16th and 17th centuries, Turkey was a very powerful country. But after defeats by Austria and Russia, they realized their only solution was modernization. You may recall how many difficulties they faced. When Napoleon's government came after the French Revolution, the Turks planned to reach India and even considered helping Tipu Sultan. The real reason was Napoleon wanted to control the Swiss Canal and conquer the Ottoman Empire. But the empire fell because the Turks lacked modern sciences, were embroiled in internal wars and conspiracies, and had very low literacy rates. They were simply not equipped to face the Industrial Revolution.

Our biggest problem as Muslims has been artificially imposed geographic boundaries limiting knowledge and awareness. We rejected Roman philosophy in religion, causing intellectual backwardness, while Western scholars prolonged Christianity's dominance. This damage was due to Ghazali's Ash'ari thought, as we did not allow Avicenna (Ibn Sina) and other Mutazilite philosophies to flourish, thus scientific thought could not develop and our society could not be built on modern foundations. We fell far behind Western societies. Meanwhile, our clerics exhausted their energy promoting life after death to hide their intellectual weaknesses and failures from us.

Dr. Muhammad Shahzad:

Can secularism ever come to Pakistan? Or can the people who are working hard for secularism in Pakistan ever see their dream fulfilled?

Dr. Baland Iqbal:

Can Pakistan ever become a secular state? Is this not a madman's dream? Shahzad, let me ask you this: Suppose tomorrow a political party comes into power, having won a large number of votes, and its manifesto promises to bring secularism—do you think that is actually possible? Can they really amend Pakistan's constitution? You know, this question was formally asked once to Mian Saqib Nisar, and his answer was 'No.' According to him, even without a referendum, it is not possible.

But I believe things are possible, although it is not necessary to view them strictly from that perspective. Look, this entire concept of secularism is based on Western experience, and every state's experience can be different—meaning every country has its own geography, economy, and political structure. We cannot compare one state's experience with another's; for instance, we cannot compare the Ottoman Empire with England or Egypt with India.

We have to keep in mind whether Christian moral values influenced their secular experience or not. Fine, then you can say that Islam is a complete code of life, and within the religion of Islam, both values—

secular and spiritual—are included, as Muhammad Ali Jinnah said. Islam cares for humans' material needs as well as their spiritual requirements. Similarly, we need a just and comprehensive society for all affairs.

This is a highly respectable idea and Islam can do this. So why insist on calling it 'secularism' and nothing else? Why not call it 'Islamic brotherhood'? That is, we want 'Islamic brotherhood,' meaning we want to live with Islamic secularism. In this way, we can implement Islamic brotherhood without changing the constitution.

Look, if change can happen in Saudi Arabia, Turkey can transform, Egypt can have a revolution, Iran can change 180 degrees, then why not true Islamic brotherhood in Pakistan? Why call it the dream of a madman?

This mind must be kept at the lowest level of moral superficiality

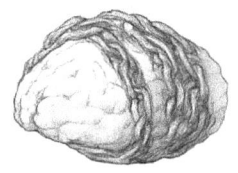

Dr. Muhammad Shahzad:

In our society, a child born into a particular family is compelled to adhere to that family's religious traditions. If the child opposes these traditions or is non-religious, it has been observed that such children are instilled with fear of shirk (polytheism), especially the severe punishments of hell. Generally, these children are viewed negatively within the family as well. So, Doctor, my first question in this regard is: How do you perceive the physiological, psychological, and social nature of the relationship with ethics?

Dr. Baland Iqbal:

Shahzad, this is a very important point. We must understand this distinction because generally, when people speak of religion in the world, they are actually thinking about ethics. For them, religion and ethics are not two different things. After all, religion tells us what is good and what is bad in this world. How should a person live according to God's command? Look, the concept of God's command and the idea of goodness are not two separate entities; they constitute one and the same thing. Just as the concept of God and the code of conduct are two names for the same entity.

High moral principles, religious duties and worship, places of worship such as mosques, temples, churches, the sense of meaning, and the meaning of life—what are all these? Think: when someone is going through the hardest times, like the loss of a loved one, what happens? People begin to think about goodness and the afterlife—what good deeds will take them to heaven, etc. So, the constitution of all these is the same: a divine concept of life, a blind belief, a sacred divine idea that is completely tied to ethics, goodness, and reward.

Now, if we separate this from ethics and think about ethics philosophically—what exactly is ethics? We come to realize that ethics is a deeply philosophical topic about how a human should live the life they have been given. Its fundamental question is: how should a person react to different situations or circumstances in life? Obviously, there is logic, arguments, and reasoning. On one side, there is blind faith and divine belief; on the other, there are arguments, logic, and rational debate. Human history is filled with this debate because each person's logic and reasoning is objective to themselves but subjective to society and others.

We connect ethics with the divine or revelation theories, which are based on universal principles or universal laws—both fixed and faith-based. In other words, we are mixing two different things. When analyzing ethics from a social perspective, we find the concept of 'Deontology,' which is essentially a religious concept derived from religion—such as the Ten Commandments in Judaism and Christianity, and similarly in Islam through the Quran. These are clear, simple, black-and-white principles: respect your parents, honor your elders, do not lie, do not steal, do not shed blood, do not kill, do not cheat, etc.

However, when we view ethics socially, we encounter 'Utilitarianism,' which asks: whenever we perform any action in life, what kind of results does it bring? Does it produce more positive or negative consequences? Does it increase pain, suffering, and difficulty, or does it provide lasting happiness? Utilitarianism can be positive or negative. Clearly, this is a practical world view of ethics, very different from the absolute black-and-white religious laws. Often, they conflict. These are the very issues that appear throughout human history, prompting debates about which path is better for humanity.

Utilitarianism, a theory recently developed by John Stuart Mill in the 19th century, focuses on positive utilitarianism—a conception of a better and more desirable life. The point is that faith is static: it offers the same principles at all times and cannot be challenged or critiqued. Its universal laws do not fit the changing scales of human life in a changing world. Ethics connected to this evolving world also changes shape.

So, can a constantly evolving ethics be based on fixed, immutable ethical principles? That's why I initially said we must understand this distinction—how religion can help regulate our changing ethics.

Dr. Muhammad Shahzad:

Doctor Iqbal, why is it that a religious person, despite practicing religion all their life, does not become an ideal or at least a good person? We Muslims have been practicing Islam for the last fourteen to fifteen hundred years, so by that measure, our society should have become exemplary by now. Considering the distinction, you described between religious ethics and subjective or objective ethics, why then have we failed to become better moral individuals or a better society—both individually and collectively?

Dr. Baland Iqbal:

Yes, Shahzad, this is a very important question. A thousand or fifteen hundred years is a long time. So, it's no excuse to say, "Oh no, society or the individual did not improve because religion was not properly practiced; otherwise, our religious ideology is flawless." Look, this kind of evasive talk is unacceptable. We must speak honestly and intellectually. Anyone who utters such things either lives in a fool's paradise or deliberately withholds the truth due to blind faith or ideology.

The reality is that there are loopholes and flaws somewhere. To find out where the problem lies, a psychological and philosophical analysis of religious ethics is essential.

Look, Shahzad, this is exactly the issue that Plato addressed in his *Euthyphro* dialogue with Socrates. Socrates asks: Is something good because it is inherently good, or is it good because God wills it? He says there is a difference because if something is good just because God wills it, then God's option is primary. But if it is good by its own nature, then God's option is secondary. That means something would still be good even if God did not exist. From here, ethics takes on a completely different form.

Let's look at literature. Dostoevsky wrote in one of his novels that if you remove God, then humans would feel free to do anything, and ethics would become completely orphaned. Psychologically, Freud had a different take: morality from God never comes alone; it comes with judgment, and at its core are shame and guilt. These feelings of shame and guilt, tied to reward and punishment and heaven and hell, cause severe psychological trauma. Healing from this trauma is almost impossible. The ego is profoundly damaged.

Hence, a religious person, when slightly distanced from the concept of God or when given "chance," fulfills their animalistic instincts or does what brings them pleasure or material gain. The problem with the judgment system is its weakness because shame and guilt are highly unpleasant emotions that people generally avoid or do not want to feel. You know many people reject God precisely because they don't want to live with those feelings.

Now, if you look at modern philosophical ideas like Nietzsche's, he calls such ethics 'slave morality.' Historically, this came from ancient Greek society, which was divided into masters and slaves—the powerful and the weak. Slaves, for survival, were submissive, obedient, and faithful to their masters, who ruled with bravery, courage, and confidence. The slaves' ethics were necessary for their survival. This slave morality was later incorporated into Christianity, which was a religion for the poor, the weak, the orphans, and the needy, with Jesus as their divine guide. So, from their perspective, these ethics were good—but in truth, they were slave morality.

According to Nietzsche, Western nations cannot progress with such slave morality, nor can it produce a fully developed, powerful, morally strong person. Such morality does not produce ego or the strength needed for a 'superman' or complete human because the feelings of shame and guilt destroy that strength.

Richard Dawkins goes a step further, saying that if you look at the post-Christian, Islamic, and Jewish historical framework, there is a great intellectual dishonesty. Many religious rules were not originally as strict or rigid; they were actually quite secular. But over time, many changes were made to make them softer and more flexible.

For example, Adolf Hitler and the Nazis were Christians, and during the Holocaust, they killed millions. What was their mentality? This antisemitism? Did they feel remorse or shame? No, because they considered it a sacred duty. Many such "righteous acts" exist in religious history. This is called 'sick ethics,' unfortunately imported by religion. It is a diseased mentality that questions the religious definition of ethics.

A major ongoing discussion revolves around why religious people fail to develop good character. In my opinion, the answer lies in these psychological and philosophical reasons.

Dr. Muhammad Shahzad:

Doctor Iqbal, our third question comes from a friend of ours, Faiz-ur-Rahman, who asked me through my mediation. He wants to know: Without religion, where can the standards of morality come from?

Dr. Baland Iqbal:

Faiz-Ur-Rahman has asked a very interesting and important question. At first glance, it seems our society, despite being religious, is one of the most corrupt societies where all kinds of evil occur day and night. The interesting thing is that mosques are full of worshippers day and night. Let's do one thing: let's set aside the major Western political powers for a moment and instead consider an example of a state or country not entangled in political issues—say Denmark. You know Denmark has the least religious people in the world compared to any religious country. Their churches are generally empty; religious beliefs there are very "liquid" or "watery." In other words, the general public in Denmark does not believe Jesus to be a prophet or the son of God but rather considers him a virtuous man who sought to bring positive change to society. They regard the Bible as a book written by humans, not a divine scripture, and miracles are seen as mere stories they often recount with a smile. They are completely detached from religious politics, and even if they try to engage, they cannot become a political force because so few people are religious there. Furthermore, an anti-religious political force cannot arise either, because that too does not interest the general public enough to gain traction.

The morality they possess is personal and individual, independent of religion. Now, what are the conditions there? A friend of mine who has lived there for a long time says that Denmark's health system and social welfare are such that doctors do not charge for treatment, similar to Canada but even more comprehensive. Since many people do not own cars, besides school buses, taxis for children—especially for going to school—are also provided free. And this is not a favor by taxi drivers but the government pays them for this service. Therefore, people happily go home and take their children to school because not only are they paid, but all government benefits support this service. Due to the heavy traffic system, people commute by bicycle just like cars; no distinction is made in standards, and traffic rules apply equally. Beggars or homeless people are hardly seen on the streets, unlike in the US and Canada. Crime rates are very low, and unemployment is minimal.

So, where does the sense of contentment and happiness come from in a society where religion is not actively practiced? It is not that such societies do not face political and social challenges—they certainly do—but the difference is that their solutions come through reason and rationality, logic, debate, discussion, and practical methods, not merely through faith, worship, speeches, or exhortations. These conditions are not unique to Denmark; if you go to Sweden, you will find similar circumstances, and even in the East, for example Japan, you will see similar situations. This means that a society can develop on secular foundations.

Look at the international indexes analyzing these societies' economies—you will find they are not in poor condition like our country Pakistan. What this means is that the individual's sense of contentment and happiness does not come from a religious paradigm; rather, it stems from the relationship and environment created by balancing family and work, by having a life beyond work with interests, hobbies, clubs, social interactions, theater, art, and music. They have developed a profound sense—or you could say the true meaning of life—with freedom and happiness, which is subjective to each individual. Such societies exist on this same planet where we live.

It would be incorrect to say those societies face no challenges; of course, they do, because they are global societies where people from all over the world come and bring their beliefs, traditions, and social psychologies, which include negative prejudices and other tendencies. They have democracy, equality, freedom of thought, speech, and expression, and whatever social problems arise, they are solved rationally. People there naturally love and care for their elderly parents and elders—arguably better than in our society. Unfortunately, here in our society, religious political manipulation spreads rumors even about this, with blatant lies told with gusto.

Now, philosophically, we should discuss this topic keeping existentialism in mind. We must recall Albert Camus's novel *The Stranger* (also called *The Outsider*), whose theme is that the universe and an individual have no connection; the universe exists in its own world and we live in ours. The sun is in its place, the moon in another, galaxies spread somewhere, clouds float somewhere else; there is no relationship between them and me. My good or bad does not affect them, nor do they cause storms or rain on me. What else is this but absurdism? When the protagonist in Camus's novel is imprisoned and facing the death penalty, instead of sorrow, he says, "Fine, kill me, since my birth too was just an accident."

Later, when Camus wrote *The Myth of Sisyphus*, he offered a solution to absurdism. He said if life has no meaning, then what meaning can purpose or essence have? Jean-Paul Sartre, when speaking of life's essence, responded: essence of what? Of meaninglessness? Therefore, Camus believed that Sisyphus, who was punished by the gods to endlessly roll a large boulder up a hill only for it to roll down again, represents the metaphor for everyday human life. The essence does not lie in throwing the rock over the hill but in joyfully carrying it, enjoying the effort itself. The moment Sisyphus smiles carrying the boulder toward the gods, punishment turns into reward, and the idea of divine punishment ceases. As the saying goes, "dew forms on the gods' desires." This means the purpose of life is to live it and to enjoy the struggle.

Jean-Paul Sartre also believed this but in a different manner. He said humans must develop their own essence, but this essence is judged by society—the "others" with whom a person constantly interacts. According to Sartre, the eyes of others that continuously watch you are hell itself; they either praise you or utterly reject you. This is where our morality develops: we do those deeds which benefit society or at least do good for others as well as ourselves. That, essentially, is good morality.

Dr. Muhammad Shahzad:

A question has come from another friend of mine, Dr. Aman Wazir, who wants to know that if a religious person is also a good person and is living a comfortable life, then why do we insist so much on making people think deeply? Such insistence might confuse them.

Dr. Baland Iqbal:

Yes, Shahzad, Dr. Aman Wazir's point is absolutely valid. Indeed, a religious person who is a good person—whose ethics are intertwined with their faith—and whose life is going smoothly without any problems, according to their divine principles, their life is almost perfect. What I will do is present a few "exemplary scenarios" for Dr. Aman Wazir to consider. If he finds that his divine principles resolve these issues satisfactorily according to his conscience, then this debate will end.

Suppose Dr. Aman Wazir is not a medical doctor but an anthropologist working in an ancient forest like the Amazon, where tribes have lived for thousands of years. Now imagine these tribes capture twelve innocent people and say to Aman Wazir: "You are our guest, and we want to honor you by asking you to personally kill just one of these twelve innocent people with your own hands. If you do this, we will spare the other eleven. Otherwise, all twelve will be killed."

Now, Aman Wazir must decide what to do in light of his faith, because from a religious perspective, killing a person is a grave sin. And honestly, how would he know which innocent life to take?

Let's leave this scenario aside—it's a very extreme and unique situation that may never arise in most people's lives. Fine, let's accept that, but let's look at other, more common scenarios that we encounter daily. For instance, Aman Wazir is a medical doctor and knows many Muslims are anti-abortion but at the same time support the death penalty, or many claim to be vegetarians but wear leather shoes and jackets. Doesn't this raise some contradictory thoughts?

Setting religious matters aside, many people identify as socialists and talk day and night about equality in society and education, yet they send their children to private schools. You can easily find politicians who always speak about family values in speeches, yet are known to have extramarital affairs.

This is an individual issue, but what about people who preach environmental cleanliness yet drive large SUVs that pollute the air daily without a second thought? In such cases, ethics rarely come to mind, nor do they want to consider them.

Or there is a person who is upset by rampant thefts and crimes in the city but happily downloads music illegally or uses software through unauthorized means. Where does his ethics go then?

Or someone suffering from unemployment who, out of desperation, resorts to forging immigration papers to move to Canada, the US, or Europe. When asked why, they calmly justify their unethical act by blaming the political policies of those countries that prevented them from finding a job in their own country.

I know many religious people who engage in such rationalization day and night. So how do your divine laws reconcile with such ethical dilemmas? You often see bearded Muslims breaking red lights in a hurry to pray, countless religious and non-religious people evade income tax, and you know that much of this tax funds atomic bombs and missiles that kill many innocent lives.

Now, you consider yourself a great humanist who talks day and night about peace and brotherhood. You see taking a human life as the gravest sin. Yet suddenly, a person appears before you who has killed many people and you fear he will kill more, so you think he must die.

Our lives are filled daily with such complex and controversial situations. How do you resolve them? I don't know what Aman Wazir would do in such scenarios. Do his black-and-white divine principles immediately provide answers? If such matters are so easily resolved by him or any religious person, then well and good. But if ever they feel that they have black-and-white justifications for every moral wrongdoing and become completely habituated to ethics, then don't be surprised. Because such unthinking adherence to divine laws generally leads people to abandon true ethics, worship the whole world blindly, commit crimes worldwide without any conscience, and easily excuse their actions by saying, "I was tempted by Satan"—meaning they are not at fault, but some imaginary being called Satan is to blame.

Dr. Muhammad Shahzad:

Dr. Iqbal, the last question in this series comes from another friend, Advocate Jafar Khan. He wants to know if a person can live simultaneously with faith and rationality.

Dr. Baland Iqbal:

Shahzad, please convey my thanks to Jafar Sahib. Look, faith comes in two forms—religious and non-religious. Religious faith is somewhat more important because whenever we hear about faith or belief, we automatically think of religious faith. Let me briefly touch on this.

The entire history of human civilization, from ancient Rome to Plato, Socrates, Aristotle, and then to the Middle Ages with St. Thomas Aquinas and St. Augustine, and even into the fifteenth century and beyond, involved attempts to prove God's existence or divine faith through rationality. You might recall Aquinas's five proofs that argued God's existence could be demonstrated through reason. This dialogue continued through Darwinism and existentialism, with German and British philosophy entangled in debates until American pragmatism in the twentieth century. This discourse on faith and reason has remained a favorite topic among scholars and philosophers for thousands of years.

Can a person live simultaneously with religion and rationality? To put it simply, if you remove reason from faith, religion becomes nothing but superstition—like believing a broken mirror will bring seven years of bad luck, or a black cat crossing your path will cause disaster, or that crows in the sky foretell divine punishment. These are superstitions—explanations without reason that have no real basis.

There are many such superstitions in religion. Whenever a religious person lacks reason, they tend to become mere religious superstitious believers.

Now, if you discard religion and live only by reason, two things can happen: one, a person leans toward nihilism, rejecting not only God but the meaning of life itself. Then they must grapple with nihilism's next stage and create meaning for life themselves, known as existentialism. Obviously, this existential challenge is not easy for everyone to bear, so an average mind prefers the comfort of religious belief, while a more scholarly mind chooses the discomfort of questioning and thought.

Similarly, there is non-religious faith developed on reason, which is essential to some extent. For example, you have faith in science that its observations and experiments will yield the most accurate possible results. This is because the edifice of scientific faith is built on the pillars of reason, and its success has only strengthened reason and faith.

When you board an airplane, you don't worry about your life despite the possibility of a crash because there are rational explanations behind safety. Or you accept an unfamiliar vaccine to prevent viral infections because there is reason and evidence supporting it.

Therefore, saying rationality and religious or non-religious faith are two different domains is not entirely accurate—they intersect continuously, but the ways they connect, diverge, and the results differ.

This mind must be distanced from genuine intelligence.

Dr. Muhammad Shahzad:

Doctor Iqbal, how would you define intelligence?

Dr. Baland Iqbal:

Shahzad, that's a scientific question—scientific in the sense that it concerns both the structure of the brain and the psyche.

Look, this large area at the front and side of the brain—what we call the frontal and temporal lobes—is directly related to our intelligence. The grey matter within these lobes houses our short-term and long-term memory capacities. It is through these very lobes that we deal with situations, whether good or bad. These regions also give us the capacity to think logically, to reason.

They determine how well we know ourselves, the extent of our passion for learning, and the depth of our self-awareness. Are we capable of reasoning? What about emotional intelligence, problem-solving abilities, critical thinking skills, planning, and the ability to link simple and complex ideas together into a logical conclusion?

All of these are considered facets of general intelligence, and neurologically, they are either directly or indirectly connected to the frontal and temporal lobes.

In the early 20th century, several important theories on intelligence emerged. One notable name is Charles Spearman, who included not only memory and knowledge accumulation but also personality flexibility as components of intelligence. According to him, beyond just thinking, what truly matters is the extent to which we are able to engage in statistical and mathematical reasoning. He believed that to understand any problem in depth, one must possess visual-spatial processing—which he referred to as a part of fluid intelligence, classifying it under primary mental abilities.

Following Spearman, we encounter Louis Thurstone, who expanded on Spearman's composition of intelligence. Thurstone added the ability for deep comprehension and imagination to the concept of intelligence—coining terms like verbal comprehension and spatial visualization.

Another significant figure is Howard Gardner, who connected intelligence with culture and civilization, recognizing that our surroundings are shaped by cultural values. He introduced the novel concept of kinesthetic intelligence, which refers to physical coordination and body control as a form of intelligence.

He also emphasized intrapersonal intelligence—how well we know ourselves, the extent of our self-awareness, and how deeply we understand our values, beliefs, and faith.

Beyond intrapersonal awareness, Gardner emphasized the role of interpersonal intelligence—our ability to understand the people around us, their temperaments, our emotional connections with them, and our behavioral responses.

He also introduced the idea of naturalistic intelligence, which involves our awareness of and engagement with nature—our understanding of mountains, rivers, animals, forests, oceans, and the natural world around us, as well as our contribution to its preservation.

Then he moved even further to include the world of language and music in the scope of intelligence. He categorized these as linguistic intelligence and musical intelligence, referring respectively to sensitivity to the meaning of words, and to rhythm and sound.

Apart from Gardner, another key figure is Robert Sternberg, who extended the definition of human intelligence to include artificial intelligence—suggesting that the ability to use artificial systems is a valid expression of human intelligence. Moreover, he identified the capacity to create new ideas from existing knowledge and to positively transform the world using those ideas. He termed these abilities as creative and practical intelligence.

Overall, we can say that:

- Fluid intelligence refers to the ability to create new worlds through new ideas.
- Crystallized intelligence relies on past experiences and observations rooted in older ideologies to move forward.

Shahzad, as you already know, the concept of IQ (Intelligence Quotient) was introduced by Alfred Binet. He created a standard by combining mental and biological factors. However, this model raised several reservations and biases, as it became clear that many people with high IQs made very little practical contribution either to themselves or society.

So an important question arises: Can a limited IQ also define the extent of intelligence?

Because time and again we see that people with average IQs often end up becoming agents of extraordinary, positive change in the world

Muhammad Shahzad:

Is the relationship between age and intelligence really as simple as people often make it out to be? As the saying goes, "You'll understand when you grow older."

Dr. Baland Iqbal:

That's a very intriguing question, Shahzad. In our society, we frequently hear this phrase: "You're still young—when you grow older, you'll understand." But the truth is, as we age, our brain actually begins to atrophy—a condition known as *cerebral atrophy*. That is, around the age of forty, the brain slowly begins to shrink, and this process accelerates significantly by the time we reach our sixties and seventies. The earliest casualty of this process is our memory, followed by a decline in our capacity to learn and comprehend. In other words, the older we grow, the more our cognitive abilities tend to diminish.

However, this brings us to a related but distinct concept: *wisdom*. People often associate wisdom with life experience and observation. But there's a crucial difference between intelligence and wisdom—specifically, the depth of understanding of the "how" and "why." I believe wisdom is a kind of metaphysical feature.

There's a story about Alexander the Great that illustrates this. He once visited a philosopher who was lying in a garden, basking in the sun. During their conversation, Alexander inadvertently stepped between the sun and the philosopher. While expressing his desire to gain some wisdom from him, the philosopher calmly said, "I'll gladly give you some wisdom, but first, kindly move out of the sunlight. Do not block from me what you cannot give."

Another example comes from the life of the Buddha. A grieving woman approached him, weeping, and said, "Something terribly unjust has happened—my beloved child has died. You claim to be wise—why can't you bring him back to life?" The Buddha replied, "I will help you, but first you must do something for me." The woman eagerly agreed. The Buddha said, "Very well—go to every house in the village and bring me the names of all the mothers who have never experienced death in their household, so I can revive all their children along with yours." As she went from home to home, she realized that nearly every household had experienced death. She came to understand that she was not alone in her grief—that death is a universal and inevitable part of life wherever there is life.

Now, coming to the modern scientific understanding of intelligence: numerous studies have been conducted on the subject. In one such study, 318 participants were categorized by age: 15–20, 20–40, 40–60, and 70+. Researchers mapped their *fluid* and *crystallized* intelligence using a triangular model rather than a horizontal or vertical graph. The findings showed that younger individuals tend to possess more *fluid intelligence*, which is linked to novel problem-solving and learning new things. In contrast, older individuals often exhibit *crystallized intelligence*, which stems from accumulated knowledge and experience.

But this raises the question: what kind of intelligence is essential for wisdom, and how much of it is necessary? Clearly, wisdom cannot be acquired through credentials or degrees. It's a unique phenomenon. A fascinating scientific study by Sharon Ryan from the University of Virginia sheds light on this. In her article, she references Socrates, who famously said, "I know that I do not know." She interprets this as an expression of *intellectual humility*—an acknowledgment of the limits of one's knowledge. But she goes further, suggesting that this also represents *epistemic accuracy*, meaning that one should know the precise boundaries of their knowledge.

Ryan argues that true wisdom isn't just about knowing your limits—it also requires deep and wide-ranging understanding of life's various dimensions. This knowledge must be so thorough that one can reach a level of certainty and even claim that they have grasped the essence of many aspects of life. But even then, can one confidently claim to be wise? Can one say they are living a "good" life?

That brings us to a crucial question: what do we mean by a "good life"? Do we mean a morally upright life? We know of many intellectuals who seem wise in their understanding of life yet are indifferent to ethics in their personal lives. So perhaps being wise is less about moral righteousness and more about rational clarity. If you can logically analyze emotions—and indeed all life options—you might still be considered wise, even if you are emotionally distant or "cold."

In earlier times, when we spoke of a wise person, we referred to someone capable of analyzing human psychology, philosophy, literature, and the social sciences. But in modern times, the criteria have shifted. Today, we evaluate wisdom through psychological and scientific parameters.

For instance, German developmental psychologist Paul Baltes conducted a study on the components of wisdom. He identified five key elements:

1. Procedural Rich Knowledge—practical experience about life.
2. Factual Rich Knowledge—deep, accurate knowledge of life matters.
3. Understanding-Rich Knowledge—a strong capacity to comprehend complexities.
4. Awareness-Rich Knowledge—a values-based awareness of broader contexts.
5. Competence in Dealing with Uncertainty—the ability to recognize and navigate ambiguity.

According to Baltes, these elements generally develop between the ages of 13 and 25. From 25 to 75, they tend to remain stable. After 75, a noticeable decline may occur.

Another noteworthy scholar is Monika Ardelt from the University of Florida, who offered a three-dimensional model of wisdom. She tied wisdom to personality traits, arguing that if we isolate wisdom from personality, it becomes merely intellectual or theoretical knowledge. She proposed that wisdom comprises:

1. Cognitive Awareness
2. An Extensive Desire to Learn
3. Reflection—genuine introspection free from self-bias, self-projection, and egocentricity.

In this sense, a truly wise person is one who can reflect with honesty and objectivity, devoid of prejudice or personal inclinations. Such wisdom fosters both intellectual clarity and a deep humility toward others.

Psychologist Robert Sternberg also proposed that wisdom involves balancing interpersonal, intrapersonal, and extra personal relationships. Only then can a person truly integrate into and adapt within society, or even consciously choose to shape a new and improved way of life.

In light of all this, the concept and definition of wisdom can be approached from many angles. But the central insight we gain here may also answer our original question: yes, wisdom *is* related to age—but not merely in terms of how *many* years one has lived. The crucial question is: how has one lived those years?

If a person has truly engaged with the phenomena discussed above, they can be said to possess some measure of wisdom. Otherwise, you may recall that when Mirza Ghalib was a child, he once mischievously addressed an elderly man not as a "venerable elder" but simply as an "old fellow." The man complained to Ghalib's uncle, who reprimanded him. But Ghalib replied, "I was only reminding him of a saying by Sheikh Saadi: *'Old age is a matter of intellect, not of years.'*"

Dr. Muhammad Shahzad:

What is the link between educational institutions, degrees, and intelligence? We often observe that many individuals, despite never being affiliated with any formal educational institution throughout their lives, are exceptionally intelligent and highly creative. Could you also shed light on whether creativity is related to intelligence?

Dr. BalandIqbal:

Shahzad, these are very intriguing questions: What is the relationship between education and intelligence, or between creativity and intelligence? In my view, the connection between education and intelligence is *bilateral*. For example, if a child has a high IQ, then naturally, the chances of that child acquiring education and earning academic degrees increase. However, the truth is that IQ and education are not the only determining factors.

Personality type, organization skills, determination, consistency, perseverance, encouragement, and above all, the social and familial environment—these all play a critical role. The presence of these elements significantly enhances the likelihood of achieving higher educational qualifications.

There's another angle to this: *Can education enhance IQ?* To understand this, let's consider a simple example. Imagine two six-year-old children—one born in January, the other in December. Since they are both technically six years old, they are placed in the same first-grade class. However, due to the eleven-month age gap between them, by the time they reach second grade, the younger child may actually demonstrate an IQ equal to or even slightly higher than the older one.

A scientific study on adults undergoing pilot training showed that those with higher IQs were able to complete their training within a month, while those with lower IQs had less than a 20% success rate. This clearly indicates two things: first, lower IQ reduces the likelihood of successfully completing such complex training; second, a person's IQ typically reaches its maximum limit during childhood. If there is any potential for further increase, it usually plateaus by the age of 30.

Even if there's a 5% chance of increasing IQ after that, it heavily depends on continuous learning. Why is that so? Because even in our schools, colleges, and universities, the primary focus of the learning process revolves around test performance—where results are mainly based on memorization.

Now, scoring well in tests also depends on certain techniques, where things like self-confidence, personality traits, and targeted preparation for specific topics often play a greater role than raw memorization or IQ. Similarly, there are some techniques to improve IQ, such as practicing puzzles or working extensively on specific subjects. So yes, there is both a direct and indirect link between IQ and educational institutions. But even if educational institutions were to provide optimal cognitive training, the overall impact on IQ would still be limited to around 5%. This has been substantiated by several scientific studies.

Now, let's turn to the relationship between creativity and intelligence. To understand this, we need to revisit Sternberg's theories on creative and analytical intelligence. He posits that the primary aim of formal education is to provide new knowledge and facilitate its memorization so that it can be applied to solve academic problems analytically. This kind of learning increases basic IQ only marginally—around 5%.

After that comes the domain of *creative intelligence*, where one develops the ability to solve imaginative and innovative problems. It is at this stage that individuals begin to generate new concepts and envision entirely new worlds based on those ideas.

From this perspective, we encounter three types of intelligence:

1. *Analytical Intelligence*
2. *Creative (Creational) Intelligence*
3. *Practical Intelligence*

Some people may be naturally gifted in certain types more than others. For example, *practical intelligence*—often referred to as *street smartness*—is a form of intelligence that doesn't always show up in academic settings but plays a crucial role in real-world problem-solving.

These three types of intelligence form a kind of interdependent circle, collectively enhancing the overall intellectual process. Interestingly, in certain individuals, these types can manifest in varying degrees. For instance, someone who is strong in *practical intelligence* may not score as high in traditional IQ tests as someone with more academic or creative intelligence.

I believe the distinction between analytical and creative intelligence also lies in the difference between *convergent* and *divergent thinking*. Creative individuals tend to think divergently—they think "outside the box," unconstrained by conventional boundaries. In contrast, those with academically grounded intelligence often rely on *convergent thinking*. They acquire knowledge within a specific field and continue to develop their intelligence within that same domain. They typically solve established problems using established methods—within the confines of the academic "box."

That's why highly educated, degree-holding individuals often become conditioned to think within structured parameters, even though their IQs may be quite high—sometimes even higher than those of creative thinkers.

In essence, intelligence isn't a one-dimensional quality. It's a multidimensional construct with several distinct forms—each valuable in its own right, each shaped by both nature and environment.

Dr. Muhammad Shahzad:

Dr. Iqbal, what is your perspective on Emotional Intelligence? Do you see it as a divine gift or a curse? In other words, what are the positive and negative aspects of emotional intelligence?

Dr. Baland Iqbal:

Shahzad, emotional intelligence has become quite popular in the modern world, especially in today's stress-ridden and anxiety-filled environment. Our awareness of our emotions is often limited, yet it's crucial to understand how emotions are connected to our stress levels. How can we regulate them through thoughtful communication? How do emotions manifest in relation to the feelings and sensitivities of others?

Emotions play a pivotal role not only in family relationships but also within communities, schools, colleges, workplaces, and across social and interpersonal domains. At the core of emotional intelligence lies *self-awareness*—the ability to recognize one's own emotions and understand how these emotions shape behavior and reactions. This insight allows a person to discern their own strengths and weaknesses. Once self-awareness is established, the next key element is *self-management*: how one expresses emotions with control and restraint.

In today's world of social media, we see people reacting impulsively—often without any self-regulation. A mere critique of their ideology or a revered personality can lead them to erupt with verbal abuse, losing all composure. In such instances, meaningful dialogue becomes nearly impossible, and civilized discourse collapses, giving way to negativity.

So, the first element is emotional awareness, the second is controlling one's emotional strengths and vulnerabilities, and the third is *social awareness*—cultivating empathy and understanding toward others in society. This involves building relationships in a way that creates a comfortable and safe environment for everyone. For example, within an organization or a group, emotional intelligence helps members coordinate harmoniously so they feel part of a peaceful rather than chaotic space.

Emotionally intelligent individuals know how to manage relationships. They possess the tact and skill to handle difficult situations without hurting their own or others' emotions. Viewed from this angle, emotional intelligence stands on four core pillars:

1. Self-Awareness – deep emotional awareness of oneself.
2. Self-Management – regulating and constructively expressing emotions.
3. Social Awareness – empathy and emotional sensitivity toward others.
4. Relationship Management – building and maintaining emotionally healthy connections.

Now the question arises: Is emotional intelligence truly essential? Consider this—while IQ is necessary for academic learning, EQ is often what helps a person succeed in real-world challenges. In high-pressure environments, managing emotions becomes crucial. Many academically brilliant students with high IQs struggle to perform under exam stress. Despite their knowledge, they may underperform or even fail due to poor emotional regulation.

This demonstrates that alongside IQ, *EQ is absolutely vital*. And this isn't limited to academics; it's equally important in the workplace. In fact, during job interviews, emotional intelligence is often evaluated more rigorously than IQ. Recruiters assess how quickly a candidate can adapt, how effectively they can build a positive social network, and how well they can contribute to organizational growth.

While this relates to relationships, there's more. Individuals lacking emotional control are often more prone to physical health problems—heart attacks, strokes, high blood pressure, infertility, and even premature aging. Similarly, mental health conditions like depression, anxiety, and chronic stress are more prevalent in those with low emotional intelligence.

One important point: A person with an exceptionally high IQ—perhaps a successful professional, scholar, or creative writer—may not necessarily be emotionally intelligent. Often, such individuals fail in family or social relationships simply because they lack the ability to manage or even understand basic human emotions and passions. The takeaway here is that a *balance between IQ and EQ* is indispensable.

That said, Shahzad, while emotional intelligence has many positive applications, it's equally important to be aware of its *darker side*. Nobel laureate economist Milton Friedman once said that the power to do good also includes the power to do harm. Everything has both a light and dark side.

For instance, a shrewd politician who understands the emotional landscape of the masses can manipulate these sentiments for personal gain. By capitalizing on public emotions and vulnerabilities, such leaders rise to power. South Asian political history, particularly in Pakistan and India, is replete with examples of leaders who incited ethnic, religious, and nationalist emotions to build political empires—often exploiting the poor and naive, even constructing false legends around themselves.

Charismatic personalities, especially narcissists, are often emotionally intelligent yet self-obsessed. They masterfully play on public emotions to achieve great power—only to inflict greater harm. Australian psychologist James Brown conducted a scientific study revealing that narcissistic, charming individuals are often both seductive and emotionally intelligent. They skillfully exploit their emotional insight for personal or political agendas.

A stark example is Adolf Hitler. He practiced emotional manipulation, using his charisma to mesmerize the masses. Similar figures can be found in Pakistani politics—leaders who speak the people's language, cry with them, act like them, and create emotional bridges through drama and performance.

On a more personal level, we see similar emotional manipulation. For instance, in an extramarital affair, one partner may exploit their knowledge of the other's emotions to deceive them with sweet words and false reassurances. Similarly, a company manager may emotionally manipulate customers with catchy slogans or rumors to sell inferior products.

Despite such risks, developing emotional intelligence remains essential. The key lies in balancing it with core intelligence and using it ethically to cultivate healthier personal and social relationships.

Dr. Muhammad Shahzad:

People often use the term *"evil genius"* for Pakistanis, implying they excel in underhanded dealings. What's your view? Is "evil genius" a real phenomenon?

Dr. Baland Iqbal:

Shahzad, I believe if we objectively analyze the people of this nation, we'll find no shortage of intelligence here. And I'm not saying this out of favoritism. The European Institute of Business Administration recently conducted a study ranking 125 countries by intelligence. Surprisingly, Pakistan ranked fourth.

Consider this: Pakistani students have set records in Cambridge A and O Level exams. Arfa Karim, the world's youngest Microsoft Certified Professional at just nine years old, was from Pakistan. Babar Iqbal was also a Microsoft prodigy from Pakistan. The country ranks seventh in the world for producing the most engineers and scientists. Pakistan has one of the largest broadband internet systems globally.

Pakistan was also the first Islamic country to become a nuclear power. Its air force pilots are recognized among the world's best. In terms of humanitarianism, Abdul Sattar Edhi stands as a towering figure—an embodiment of social intelligence rarely seen anywhere else in the world. Nobel laureate Dr. Abdus Salam, a physicist, was also Pakistani. Malala Yousafzai, whether one agrees with her or not, remains an icon of resistance to terrorism and a symbol for girls' education.

Pakistan has an ancient cultural lineage that stretches back thousands of years to the Indus Valley and Mohenjo-Daro civilizations. So what then is "evil genius"?

Hand a nation over to poverty, illiteracy, overpopulation, lawlessness, terrorism, favoritism, corruption, and unemployment—then ask how intelligence is applied in such a setting. When honest avenues fail, people resort to alternative, sometimes unethical, paths. Whether we call it "evil genius" or not, the truth is these people are inherently intelligent—they are simply forced into survival through negative means. And when conditions are so dire, *any* nation can become a breeding ground for "evil genius."

This mind must be trapped in misconceptions about Islamophobia

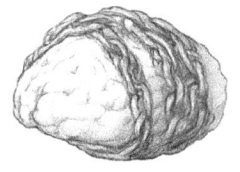

Dr. Muhammad Shahzad:

Dr. Iqbal, Islamophobia is often justified in the West, with various arguments presented in its favor, whereas from our perspective, it is viewed as a critical and condemnable stance taken by the West. So, my first question is: What exactly is Islamophobia? Is it similar to other psychological phobias, such as hydrophobia — the fear of water — or acrophobia — the fear of heights that makes people anxious on mountains or airplanes? Or claustrophobia — the fear of enclosed spaces? Or is Islamophobia more like xenophobia — a deep-seated hostility toward foreigners or outsiders, manifesting as hatred in the hearts of a local population?

Dr. Baland Iqbal:

Shahzad, your use of the word *"justify"* is quite apt because the act of providing arguments to rationalize this phenomenon is precisely what has made it so complex. Other phobias — hydrophobia, acrophobia, claustrophobia — do not require justification. If someone naturally fears water or heights, that's accepted. But Islamophobia is rooted in a multitude of historical, political, and social causes. It is less a phobia in the clinical sense and more a form of prejudice — a predisposed negative attitude or judgment against anyone who practices Islam or belongs to the Muslim community.

This prejudice leads people to view Muslims with suspicion or respond to them with hostility. It's a form of animosity and fear not unlike the aversion many Muslims feel toward Jews, or the discomfort that traditional societies have toward homosexuals — gays and lesbians. Similarly, racism works both ways — whites against blacks and blacks against whites — and has persisted for generations. Islamophobia closely resembles the racism found in nationalist circles — for example, in Pakistan, where certain people consider their ethnic group superior for no reason, or where Sindhis, Punjabis, Baloch, and Pashtuns hold prejudiced views against each other.

Historically, Germans harbored hatred against Jews before World War II. Even today, many Americans consider their race superior. Jews often believe they are God's chosen people. This mindset — of believing oneself to be inherently better than others and consequently harboring irrational hostility — is a classic example of what we call *prejudice*.

So, the anti-Muslim sentiment that is constructed and perpetuated falls under the umbrella of Islamophobia. And since it is a socially and politically driven behavior, people go to great lengths to produce arguments to legitimize it.

An interesting point to note here is that when such prejudice is directed against Jews or Hindus, it's not labeled as "Jew phobia" or "Hindu phobia." Hatred of Jews is termed *anti-Semitism*, and prejudice against Hindus is often discussed under *racism*. But Islamophobia is a peculiar term in itself. To understand it fully, we must explore the historical and social context behind it.

Whether it is Islamophobia or other types of fear, the neuroanatomical processes involved are fairly consistent. All fear responses activate certain areas of the brain — particularly the hypothalamus and the pituitary axis. When triggered, this axis releases a flood of neurotransmitters — such as epinephrine, norepinephrine, and serotonin — which generate instinctive emotional reactions instead of rational reasoning.

For example, if gunshots are heard, or a bomb explodes, the immediate assumption — based on media propaganda or past incidents — is that it must be an Islamic terrorist. Similarly, if a bomb goes off somewhere, one might reflexively think it's an Israeli conspiracy. Because these conclusions have already been preconditioned in the mind, the fear response aligns accordingly — leading to symptoms such as anxiety, palpitations, or sweating.

Dr. Muhammad Shahzad:

What is the historical background of Islamophobia? And why has it grown so much more intense over time?

Dr. Baland Iqbal:

At its core, Shahzad, Islamophobia arises from the same mindset of *"us versus them."* To understand this fully, we should look into Edward Said's work and return briefly to history.

You'll recall that after the Prophet Muhammad's passing in 632 CE, Islamic states began to expand rapidly. Islamic culture and governance spread across regions that came under Muslim control — Turkey, Persia, the Middle East, North Africa, Spain, Sicily — and by the 13th and 14th centuries, Islam had reached parts of India, Afghanistan, Indonesia, Malaysia, and much of South and Central Asia.

However, the *first significant roots* of Islamophobia in the Western psyche likely stemmed from the Crusades — a series of religious wars from the 11th to 13th centuries, during which Muslim armies attacked Western regions. This instilled a deep historical fear.

Later, during colonization, when Spanish, French, and British fleets began invading Islamic territories with imperialistic ambitions, mutual xenophobia emerged — a reciprocal fear and distrust between colonizers and the colonized.

The next turning point came with the Iranian Revolution in the late 1970s, which disrupted Western oil interests. Ayatollah Khomeini's regime posed a political threat to Western-backed monarchies like that of Reza Shah Pahlavi. From here on, Islam began to be portrayed negatively in Western media, particularly Hollywood.

Muslim characters became stereotypical *militant villains*, while American CIA agents were portrayed as saviors and defenders of humanity. Magazines like *TIME* framed Iran's revolution as an "Islamic revival" or "return of the Islamic militant." Films such as *Raiders of the Lost Ark* depicted Middle Easterners as backward, and movies like *Delta Force* showcased plane hijackings with Muslim antagonists. Books like *Clash of Civilizations* predicted that future global conflicts would be driven not by geography, but by *cultural and religious* differences.

These developments between the 1970s and early 2000s laid the groundwork. But then came September 11, 2001 — the second major wave of Islamophobia. After 9/11, Islamophobic sentiments were systematically propagated throughout the Western world. Radical groups such as Taliban, Al-Qaeda, and Daesh became household names.

Well-established Muslim states — Iraq, Iran, Syria, Afghanistan — were rebranded as hubs of extremism. Islam itself was cast as a *jihadi ideology*, and Muslims as inherent terrorists. This narrative was relentlessly pushed through both electronic and print media, causing widespread fear and hysteria. It dovetailed with the U.S.-led *War on Terror*, resulting in invasions of Iraq and Afghanistan and the establishment of places like Guantanamo Bay, where prisoners were subjected to inhumane treatment.

Unfortunately, during this time, the Western public was never allowed to feel remorse or guilt, as the media actively dehumanized Muslim war detainees — portraying them as devils and eternal enemies of humanity.

This second wave extended from 2001 to 2015. Then came the third phase, which emerged over the last five to seven years. This phase is driven largely by demographic changes due to immigration. As Muslim populations increased in European and North American countries, local populations grew anxious, leading to a rise in right-wing populist politics.

Leaders like Emmanuel Macron in France, Donald Trump in the U.S., and Narendra Modi in India harnessed this anxiety to fuel their political agendas. France passed the Anti-Separatism Bill; meanwhile, both the U.S. and India cultivated atmospheres hostile to Muslims.

All these political, social, and historical developments helped legitimize the concept of Islamophobia — not just as a feeling, but as a political strategy. It was actively disseminated via radio, TV, cinema, newspapers, magazines, pamphlets, and especially social media —

Facebook, Twitter, TikTok, WhatsApp — all of which helped create a vast Islamophobic audience.

It has been an organized and strategic campaign, executed with such precision that its results have exceeded even the most optimistic projections.

Dr. Muhammad Shahzad:

We, too, exhibit Christian-phobia, Hindu-phobia, and Jewish-phobia in our society. So, can we view these as counterparts to Islamophobia?

Dr. Baland Iqbal:

Yes, Shahzad, you're right. Similar hateful sentiments toward Christians, Hindus, and Jews are prevalent in our society as well. The only difference is that we don't label them with terms like "Hindu-phobia" or "Jewish-phobia." But terminology isn't the real issue — the core lies in our thoughts and behavior. We have our own long, grim history of persecution — even of those who follow our own religion. Take, for example, the persecution of so-called "deviant" Muslims — that is, Muslims whose faith doesn't align with a particular dominant narrative. Shia Muslims, for instance, face routine acts of violence. They are dragged off buses, identified via ID cards, and executed. Their mosques and 'Imambargahs' are targeted with bomb blasts.

Now, as for non-Muslim minorities — right after Partition, over eight million Hindus lived in what became Pakistan — more than in many parts of the Hindu-majority world. At that time, there were around 1,300 functioning temples. Today, only 30 remain operational. Consider that: when Pakistan was created, 20% of its population comprised minorities like Hindus and Christians; now that number has dropped to just 4%. This indicates they either migrated voluntarily, were forced to flee under duress, or were coerced into converting — effectively becoming Muslim by force.

Just recently, under Imran Khan's government, remember what happened? He publicly referred to Osama bin Laden as a martyr of Islam. At the same time, in this age of space exploration and technology, he was planning a return to a 7th-century Madina model of governance. During his tenure, there was even a proposal to build a Shri Krishna Temple in Islamabad for the welfare and inclusion of religious communities. But when the bill reached the Assembly, it was vehemently opposed by Chaudhry Pervaiz Elahi. Then Jamia 'Ashrafia' issued a fatwa saying no temple could be built in an Islamic state. Mufti Taqi Usmani added the argument that regardless of what is built there, what matters is what kind of worship will take place there.

Go to YouTube and search "Shri Krishna Mandir Islamabad" — you'll likely find a barren plot of land where some "soldier of Islam" is standing and calling the adhan. This paints a vivid picture of how well we've cared for the places of worship of our minorities.

And the rest? Visit the slums where impoverished Christian and Hindu communities live. Look into the killings committed under the pretext of blasphemy, the forced conversions and marriages of Hindu women, and those who are kidnapped and raped if they refuse to convert. You'll find all of this, unfortunately, in our so-called pure Islamic society. The only thing you'll feel in response is shame. Ironically, while we continuously present moral and religious lectures on media platforms, these political and religious declarations are little more than farcical rhetoric.

In reality, a practical form of Christian-phobia and Hindu-phobia is deeply rooted in Muslim societies. And if you still doubt what I'm saying, just look at the historical events from the past 20 years. In 2005, a burnt page of the Qur'an was found blowing through the streets of a Christian neighborhood in Faisalabad. In response, mobs torched dozens of Christian homes. In 2009, 40 more homes were burned in Gujranwala. In 2013, a church in Peshawar was bombed, killing 80 people. In 2015, another attack on a church killed 14 and injured 70. In 2017, yet another church was attacked, burning nine people alive.

There's an entire list of such events — like the case of Rimsha Masih, who was relentlessly pursued, and Asia Bibi, whose ordeal exposed the hollowness of religious leaders' claims of Islamic peace and unity to the whole world. Surely, the world notices the hypocrisy between our words and our actions. That's why when slogans against Islamophobia are raised in the West, they often respond with a knowing smirk, thinking: *"We know just how much Hindu-, Jewish-, and Christian-philia exists in your part of the world."*

Dr. Muhammad Shahzad:

Pakistan's political parties frequently use the slogan of Islamophobia to serve their political ends. Why do they repeatedly find the need to exploit it? Do Muslims or Islam gain anything from this political maneuvering?

Dr. Baland Iqbal:

Shahzad, in Pakistan, political parties function largely on advertising slogans and superficial rhetoric. These are crafted to gather as many voters as possible and to feed the belly of a hollow democracy so they can seize power through electoral politics. The "face value" of such slogans lies in securing votes and governing power — they have no substantial or practical worth.

Therefore, these slogans have no real impact. But of course, political parties put considerable thought into formulating them and then hand them over to political marketers to avoid any major backlash. These slogans are crafted in an *artistic* way — designed to be catchy, emotionally resonant, and easily memorized by the masses. They often carry poetic rhythm, musicality, and, beneath the surface, all the toxins of hate — so that they echo in people's minds at least until election day.

This phenomenon is even more visible today in the era of social media, where populist leaders frequently engage in such practices. For instance, Macron in France appeases the right wing by stoking Islamophobia and anti-immigration sentiments to attract voters. Similarly, Donald Trump in the U.S. has relied on American nationalism, promising to "make America great again," while portraying immigrants as threats to American culture and safety, and as causes of unemployment — narratives that strongly appeal to right-wing and fundamentalist factions.

In Pakistan, Imran Khan employed shallow populist rhetoric, swinging between the dream of a Madinia state and superficial liberalism to enlarge his vote bank. Likewise, Narendra Modi in India has built his entire political project over the past decade on a Hindu-nationalist front against Muslims. These populist leaders create highly polarized and extremist environments. Such narratives spread quickly because they are emotionally charged, deeply polarizing, and — unfortunately — very appealing.

They especially resonate with youth and politically immature minds. But aside from benefiting the leaders themselves, these slogans do more harm than good — damaging national economies and international relations.

Dr. Muhammad Shahzad:

So, is Islamophobia simply a commodity to be sold in capitalist societies?

Dr. Baland Iqbal:

Indeed, political parties reap the political and economic benefits of Islamophobia, while the costs are invariably borne by the public. History shows us this pattern clearly. After the first half of the 20th century, once World War II ended and Hitler was defeated, the Allied powers — initially united — began turning against each other. This gave rise to the anti-Communist campaign.

Later, when the Communist bloc began to collapse, Islamism became the new target. The irony is striking: the very same "oppressed jihadi Islam" that once fought the godless Communists was now rebranded overnight as the "tyrannical militant Islam" threatening capitalist powers. In short, the symbol of fear shifted from red to green — from the communist red to Islamic green. The nature of the conflict between "kufr and Islam" was flipped entirely.

All of this was done for political and economic advantage. There was no real threat to Islam before, nor is there any today. These are all political marketing techniques — low-cost, high-return strategies. After decolonization, we witnessed a shift toward indirect colonization. Control slipped from the hands of the European empires (France, Britain, Spain, Portugal) into those of capitalist powers like the United States. These powers used the very jihadi forces they had supported during the Cold War against new geopolitical rivals like China and India. Simultaneously, destabilizing Middle Eastern nations socially and politically made them easier to control economically.

Even within the West, immigrant issues are manipulated for political gain. Often, just a single shooting at a mosque or a street explosion is enough to incite public fear. In some cases, religious groups themselves unwittingly or willingly participate in this spectacle.

One consequence of this is that even if Muslim immigrant populations grow demographically, they never emerge as a serious political force, because a negative image constantly trails them. They're perceived as a perpetual threat to local populations. In short, Islamophobia is a multi-purpose tool — a bow that shoots arrows in many directions, politically and economically efficient, and incredibly effective in perpetuating fear and division.

This mind must be kept unaware of the reality of the marriage system.

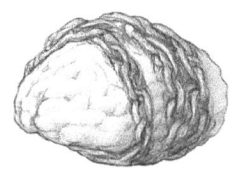

Dr. Muhammad Shahzad:

Could you enlighten us about the historical and foundational background of the marriage system?

Dr. Baland Iqbal:

Shahzad, *marriage* is a fascinating yet serious social subject that, unfortunately, is seldom discussed in depth. The institution of marriage has a long history, with evidence dating back nearly 4,500 years. Even during the hunter-gatherer era, some form of marriage system existed, albeit in a very different form. In those early tribal societies, formal one-on-one marriages were uncommon. Instead, groups of 25–30 individuals formed marital collectives, living as one extended familial unit, where wives were shared among members. This communal form of marriage persisted until around 2,000 years before the birth of Jesus Christ.

Society, however, began to evolve, and with it, the norms and structures of marriage. We find historical documentation in ancient Mesopotamian societies—like the Akkadian, Sumerian, and Babylonian Empires—showing how marriage gradually shifted from communal relationships to more individualized contracts. In these later societies, a man often kept multiple wives, concubines, and even young male partners to fulfill his sexual desires, all sanctioned by law.

A significant shift occurred when religion—particularly organized religion—began integrating its rituals into marriage. Religion introduced a spiritual dimension, rendering marriage a sacred tradition. When the Catholic Church became intertwined with state power, marriage evolved into a religious and political contract. Religious morality, vows, and legal frameworks became embedded in the institution, transforming marriage into a divine covenant witnessed by God, His son, and holy scriptures. It soon became the foundation of the state's family structure and a means to preserve a woman's honor and dignity.

Over time, legal reforms also incorporated property rights into the marital agreement, further solidifying the institution. Even in

Mesopotamian society, during wedding festivals, a father would formally "give away" his daughter, stating that he did so "so their children may have legal and religious rights." In other societies—such as Persian or pre-Islamic Arab cultures—marriage was essentially a contract over ownership, where women were regarded as men's property. These agreements allowed men and women to live together, but without formal protections, the system was prone to abuse.

Before the advent of the Prophet Muhammad, the tribes surrounding the Arabian Peninsula were steeped in tribal warfare, plunder, and regression. Women were often treated as spoils of war, bought and sold like commodities. These transactions, too, involved contracts, but they did little to dignify the status of women. Following the Prophet's passing in the 7th century, when the Islamic system was established across the Arabian Peninsula, it bore resemblance to the Church-state structures of medieval Europe. Like Catholic canon law, Islamic Sharia became legally binding, giving marriage a formal legal standing.

As for romance and love, these were later incorporations into the marriage system, likely during the medieval period. In fact, the romantic dimension is rooted more in French cultural traditions, which eventually integrated into marriage. A well-known example is the 13th-century affair between King Arthur's wife and Lancelot in Britain. Literary works of that time—poetry, fables, and novels—also began emphasizing female beauty and love, gradually influencing the concept of marriage.

So, while religion sanctified marriage, romance brought respect and social esteem to women. According to Marilyn Yalom's *History of the Wife*, before the idea of romantic love entered marriage, women largely served men and catered to their whims. But with the emergence of romantic ideals, it was men—Prince Charming—who began serving women's emotional needs.

Now, when we turn to the American context, it too was not always progressive. Until 1907, American law stated that if a woman married a foreign man, she would lose her U.S. citizenship. It wasn't until much later that this law was overturned. Until 1920, women didn't even have the right to vote. The feminist movement dramatically shifted these norms—granting women not only voting rights but also new marital rights. In the 1970s, legislation addressed issues like property distribution and sexuality in marriage. Stephanie Coontz, in her book *The Way We Never Were: American Families and the Nostalgia Trap*, argues that the last 40 years have seen more radical changes in the marriage system than in the previous 5,000 years.

Dr. Muhammad Shahzad:

Would you say that marriage is a natural or entirely unnatural process? In your view, what political, social, or religious factors made marriage an essential component of society?

Dr. Baland Iqbal:

I don't believe marriage is a natural process at all. It is, in essence, a deeply social and cultural construct. Efforts have been made to present it as natural, primarily to shape society in a particular structural way. Religion, culture, psychology, customs, laws, and morality—many elements have been grafted onto it, but at its core, the structure of marriage is built upon three major sociological truths.

The first is anthropological: though men and women are psychologically different, their complementarity appears to be a natural function.

The second is biological: reproduction cannot occur without the union of man and woman.

The third is social: both parents are essential for the healthy social development and upbringing of a child.

These truths are why governments provide legal support to marriage—to ensure future generations are raised in stable, healthy environments. Since religious individuals view religion as a natural process, they consequently consider marriage, when linked with religion, to be a natural act. For them, divine approval makes marriage a "sacred bond."

When romance was added to the equation, marriage became more than a *sexual, religious, or legal contract*; it evolved into a "bond of love." However, this created a philosophical and psychological dilemma: how do we distinguish between sexual desire and romantic love when the biological and neurological underpinnings of both are nearly identical? Both release neurotransmitters like dopamine, norepinephrine, serotonin, and oxytocin, and activate similar brain regions—thalamus, hypothalamus, amygdala, and the limbic system—similar to addiction cycles.

Fascinatingly, Western studies found that in marriages lasting 3–4 years, the ventral pallidum—a brain region associated with reward—shows increased receptor activity for vasopressin, a bonding hormone. This may explain why such marriages are emotionally harder to break.

So, what, then, is the real difference between love and sex? In my view, true love prioritizes your partner's well-being above your own. When someone cares more for their partner than for themselves, that bond transcends mere sexual attraction and becomes a metaphysical connection.

To understand how marriage is formed, maintained, and damaged, we must also consider Abraham Maslow's Humanistic Theory. He argues that human beings are active participants in their life journey, seeking *self-actualization*. Life becomes a hierarchy of needs—from basic physiological needs like food and shelter, to safety, to love and belonging, and finally to self-actualization—where one becomes the fullest version of oneself. At the pinnacle is *self-transcendence*, the desire to go beyond oneself for a higher purpose.

Marriage forms a crucial pillar in this hierarchy. If someone experiences divorce, the entire framework of their self-actualization can collapse. The trauma is profound. That's why many avoid divorce or separation. Even if a relationship becomes strained, people often stay together—for societal reasons, for their children, or simply to avoid emotional disintegration.

This is why many relationships become *social marriages*—maintained only for appearances or the children's well-being. Another major factor is economic security. In South Asian societies like Pakistan or India, many women are homemakers and realize they may struggle to survive without their husband's financial support. Moreover, these are patriarchal societies—religiously and socially—where women's rights are constantly under threat. The situation is so dire that sometimes single, divorced, or widowed women hang a man's jacket at home or record a male voice message on their phones just to create the illusion of male presence for safety.

As Maslow notes, one major reason for the survival of marriage is fear—the fear of growing old or dying alone. Many couples choose to stay together in old age out of this fear of loneliness. Another factor is psychological flexibility—successful couples are often willing to change and adapt for each other.

In conclusion, marriage is less a natural instinct and more a social structure built to maintain stability. It adapts with time, reshaped by culture, politics, economy, and emotional needs.

Dr. Muhammad Shahzad:

Doctor Iqbal, is there any connection between the patriarchal structure of marriage and the capitalist system?

Dr. Baland Iqbal:

Yes, Shahzad, there is a deep and intrinsic link between the two—especially when seen through the lens of religious ideology. To understand this relationship, we must revisit history. If you consider the era of the Catholic Church and read the treatises of Saint Augustine, you'll find that his ideology regarding marriage rests on three foundational pillars: fidelity, procreation, and the sacramental role of religion. These three elements are not only central to Catholicism but are also prevalent in Judaism, Islam, and Hinduism.

What do these commonalities reveal? Fundamentally, they stem from religion. The capitalist system we practice today is essentially a *patriarchal capitalist system*. Whether it's the distribution of property, the labor structure, or broader economic and social distinctions like class divisions, marriage has been shaped within the framework of capitalism infused with religious ideology.

If you examine the fundamental development of Western capitalism, you'll notice how religion was used strategically to integrate or domesticate sovereign classes—transforming them into faithful, obedient domestic classes. Within this context, the institution of marriage played a crucial role.

The insistence on marrying within the same sect, race, profession, or socioeconomic class is essentially an effort to preserve one's identity and community—but religion is used to legitimize and naturalize these efforts. In today's computerized, modern 21st century, religion continues to be wielded as a sacred weapon within capitalism to sustain the marriage institution.

Regardless of these mechanisms, the truth remains that capitalism is perhaps the greatest enemy of genuine love. In a capitalist worldview, love is measured by capital—not by human connection. That is why the traditional system of marriage is in decline.

Dr. Muhammad Shahzad:

Given the growing trend of cohabitation without marriage in the West, what's your opinion? Is the institution of marriage disappearing entirely from Western societies?

Dr. Baland Iqbal:

That observation is largely accurate. As I mentioned earlier, the capitalist system has fundamentally shifted people's priorities. In Western societies, fewer people are choosing to marry. Divorce statistics tell a compelling story: the divorce rate for first marriages is 57%, for second marriages 67%, and for third marriages it reaches 71%.

The concept of family has also evolved. What was once a "traditional family"—a husband, wife, and two children—has now diversified. Today, families can be stepfamilies, single-parent families, or common-law partnerships. Some family structures are so fluid that they defy conventional definitions altogether.

Previously, the father was traditionally seen as the breadwinner. Now, both spouses often work to support the household, creating a shared power dynamic but also internal economic stress. In cases of marital discord or divorce, men often bear the brunt, both emotionally and financially. Consequently, for many men, marriage has become a high-risk undertaking.

Moreover, there are additional complicating factors—alcohol, drugs, sexual diversity. Society is more varied than ever: some people are lesbian, gay, transgender, or bisexual. These identities inevitably influence the institution of marriage.

Companionship itself has changed. Young people often mistake infatuation for love and rush into marriage, lacking awareness of love's deeper components—patience, sacrifice, and emotional maturity. Many marriages dissolve at the first sign of conflict due to this immaturity.

Divorce, once a taboo, is now increasingly normalized. Women's autonomy has been a positive force in enabling individuals to exit toxic relationships, but it has also contributed to the rising divorce rate.

In short, marriage is no longer seen as a sacred social contract in Western society. Over recent decades, there's been a growing perception that both capitalism and religion have artificially constructed the institution of marriage. Marriages based on wealth, status, sect, or race often lack emotional depth or romantic love, making the idea of a formal contract seem ethically questionable.

As a result, many couples in the West now prefer to live together purely for love, without formalizing the relationship through marriage.

Dr. Muhammad Shahzad:

Doctor Iqbal, what are your thoughts on lesbian and gay marriages? Also, please share your opinion on the fact that many young people today are reluctant to take on the responsibilities of marriage—especially child-rearing—and view marriage as a threat to their freedom.

Dr. Baland Iqbal:

Shahzad, if you read the Old Testament, you'll find that homosexuality—gays and lesbians—is not a new or modern phenomenon. Historical records from the lands of Canaan, the Sinai Valley, and ancient Egypt reflect this. Even in the Old Testament, Moses was instructed to prohibit his people from engaging in the practices of the surrounding nations—these prohibitions included homosexual behavior.

For example, Roman Emperor Nero famously married a young boy named Sporus after the death of his wife Sabina. This was not a secret affair—the entire city took part in the celebrations. Such unions were both socially and legally recognized in ancient times.

Fast forward to 2025: there are now 33 countries worldwide where same-sex marriages are legally recognized—including the U.S., Canada, the U.K., Australia, Sweden, Portugal, the Netherlands, Cuba, Denmark, and Mexico. Roughly 17% of the global population identifies as gay, and many have married their partners.

Religious societies often argue that the West is misusing the concept of "freedom of religion" to justify practices like polygamy, incestuous relationships, and multiple sexual partners. In contrast, Western societies defend homosexuality as a natural instinct supported by biological and scientific reasoning. Denying such individuals legal recognition, they argue, would marginalize them and subject them to systemic discrimination, which contradicts the principles of an egalitarian society.

Transgender individuals, in this context, are regarded as ordinary people who should not be relegated to the margins. In fact, studies show that adopted children raised by same-sex couples often receive better care than those raised by some heterosexual biological parents.

As for the future of marriage, five key points illustrate where things are headed:

1. Although marriage is conventionally defined as a union between one man and one woman, in reality, people frequently maintain multiple relationships. Even when monogamy is legally mandated, both men and women often engage in multiple sexual relationships—particularly in certain social classes where it is considered fashionable.
2. The idea that marriage is exclusively between a man and a woman is already obsolete. Just search online—you'll find that in over 35 countries, marriages between gay, lesbian, transgender, and transsexual individuals are legally and socially accepted.
3. The notion of lifelong commitment is increasingly fading. Even during the wedding ceremony, couples casually mention, "If it doesn't work out, we'll just get a divorce." Divorce is seen as a simple, routine outcome.
4. Marriage is no longer considered a complicated legal contract demanding lifelong commitment. Friendly divorces are common, lawyers and psychologists are readily available, and social workers assist with child welfare. Everything is streamlined.
5. As for sexual fidelity—frankly, it's almost nonexistent in both Western and Eastern societies. Online affairs, pornography, and digital distractions make true faithfulness exceedingly rare—even within the same bed.

Ask a young person today whether they plan to marry, and they'll list many prerequisites: completing their education, securing a career, going through a process of self-discovery, becoming financially independent, exploring the world, reflecting on their divorced parents' lives, and considering the overwhelming costs of raising children in an expensive world.

With all these factors in mind, marriage becomes a low-priority option. In fact, surveys show that 40% of Americans now shrug and say that the era of marriage is over.

It's quite possible that, a hundred years from now, marriage will be something we'll see displayed in museums. That's how it appears to me.

So, what happens next? Perhaps the traditional marriage system will be replaced entirely. We might see something similar to automobile lease agreements—limited-term marriage contracts, such as: "These are our shared fantasies—why not live together for four or five years and see how it goes? If it works, we'll renew the contract for another five."

Child-rearing, too, could evolve through technologies like IVF, hormonal treatments, surrogacy, and egg donation. In this new reality, inheritance laws might dissolve altogether, as the nature of parent-child relationships becomes need-based rather than ownership-based.

In that sense, it's entirely plausible that within the next century, a wholly new system of marriage will emerge—driven by open and closed social practices, personalized preferences, and evolving definitions of love and responsibility.

This mind must be confined within an artificial intelligence.

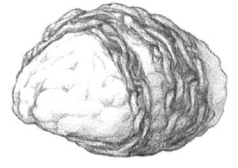

Dr. Muhammad Shahzad:

Dr. Iqbal, what is your opinion on Artificial Intelligence? What kind of impact do you think it will have on our society as a whole?

Dr. Baland Iqbal:

Yes, Shahzad, this is indeed a very important subject. In the next twenty to twenty-five years, the world around us will be dramatically transformed—perhaps even sooner. A completely new and unfamiliar world is rapidly emerging. In fact, I might be overestimating the timeline—it's possible that everything will change even faster.

We are already witnessing the effects of artificial intelligence across nearly every domain of life: transportation systems, the concept of flying cars, driverless vehicles, robotics—whether in manufacturing, sales, insurance, or healthcare. Profound changes are also visible in the social realm, and they're happening at an astonishing pace.

Take the example of China's Xiaoice chatbot—you've likely heard of it. They've managed to integrate emotional intelligence into it, enabling conversations not only on casual topics but also in areas like fine art, philosophy, religion, history, politics, and human health. You can engage in deep, intellectually rich discussions for hours with these AI agents—especially if you don't have like-minded people around. It's said that since the platform was launched, over a hundred million people have joined and continue to engage with it today.

Similarly, with platforms like ChatGPT and DeepSeek, the need for traditional professors, institutions, or academies has dramatically diminished. Whatever academic question arises in your mind, you simply type it in and receive an immediate, detailed answer.

Of course, this didn't happen overnight. Take recognition technology, for instance. Until 1995, we could only read delivery addresses on letters or parcels—maybe up to postal addresses at most. But today, we can accurately interpret street signs and navigate with astonishing precision. In linguistic recognition, we now use algorithmic image processing to identify individuals even in a crowd—and even interpret words through lip movements.

With AI, we can now generate articles automatically—so why would we still need journalists in the traditional sense? Every passing minute and hour bring forth a new AI-driven reality. In my view, the pace at which this new world is forming leaves little time before we experience a radical global transformation.

Dr. Muhammad Shahzad:

Can Artificial Intelligence play a role in fulfilling our basic human needs—like food, clothing, and shelter?

Dr. Baland Iqbal:

Undoubtedly, Shahzad. Artificial Intelligence is already playing a significant role in addressing these basic needs.

Take food, for instance. Until recently, food delivery systems—like the one in California—were flawed. Food would be produced in one place and transported vast distances: potatoes from Iowa, bananas from Costa Rica. As a result, a substantial portion of the food would go stale or be wasted.

AI has helped address these inefficiencies. One company, for example, has developed a product called Cutin, which, when sprayed on vegetables, extends their shelf life. Similarly, for centuries, agriculture was mostly horizontal—requiring vast stretches of land. But now, vertical farming is emerging. Technologies like hydroponics are enabling us to grow specific vegetables without being bound by seasons. We're now able to manipulate the growing environment itself.

In this way, AI and technology have begun to solve the food problem.

Now, about clothing: The delivery process has also been revolutionized through virtual methods. 3D printing has introduced an entirely new concept to shopping. Imagine this: you need to attend a meeting urgently and must wear a specific outfit, but you don't have the time to go to a mall. You simply put on your virtual headset, scan your body image, and tell your virtual assistant the color and texture preferences for your outfit. Instantly, various styles begin to appear on your screen. You select your preferred set, and the assistant sends the design to a nearby warehouse where it's 3D printed. In just a short while, an aerial drone delivers the outfit to your doorstep. So, clothing—just like food—is now accessible with unprecedented ease.

Now let's talk about housing.

AI has given rise to the concept of Smart Cities. With the increasing threat of global warming and extreme weather changes, population distributions are likely to shift—either from plains to mountains or from urban centers back to rural areas. In such scenarios, AI is helping envision a sustainable urban future. Data is being collected continuously to prevent greenhouse gas overconsumption and guide future planning. Artificial intelligence is, in essence, transitioning life into an entirely new mode of existence.

These changes are already becoming visible in Western societies. But soon enough, they will spread and become part of a shared human culture in the East as well.

Dr. Muhammad Shahzad:

Just as artificial intelligence is reshaping the dynamics of food, clothing, and shelter, do you think it will also play a significant role in addressing other issues like climate change, education, and healthcare?

Dr. Baland Iqbal:

Absolutely, Shahzad. You've raised a valid point. AI is indeed contributing to solutions in areas like climate, healthcare, and other complex issues. For instance, a recent study in the United States revealed that approximately 1.2 million students drop out right after high school. Now, the reason might surprise you—it turns out that many of them cited "boredom" as the main factor. They found university education dull and disengaging.

In response, numerous scientific studies were conducted to better understand and address this issue. One such study took place at an MIT lab, which led to the development of a new educational model known as the *Self-Directed Educational System*. They installed video games and books into Motorola Xoom tablets and sent these devices to remote villages in Tanzania and Ethiopia—places with no access to teachers or formal education. Astonishingly, within moments, the children figured out how to power the tablets. Soon, through self-discovery, they began exploring the installed games and books. Within months, not only did they become familiar with the educational content and songs, but some even memorized them. What's more, after about a year, some of the children learned how to hack the operating system itself.

This success prompted the XPRIZE Foundation to launch a formal global project involving around 700 teams. The leading team in that initiative remarked that if we were to replace our traditional academic systems with a self-directed model, we might be able to deliver in North America in one day what currently takes an hour in these experimental settings. In essence, this represents a transformative shift in educational philosophy. The possibility of addressing global illiteracy without schools, colleges, or institutions is now real. This is a significant and positive contribution of AI—something we simply cannot ignore.

Similarly, in the realm of global warming, AI is playing a crucial role. NASA's satellites, for instance, can detect rising temperatures in forests well before they ignite, helping prevent fires and mitigate damage. It's part of the broader shift we discussed earlier—the vision of smart cities, reducing greenhouse gas emissions, and managing pollution to create healthier environments. These technologies are not just preserving the quality of life on Earth—they're extending the very life of the planet. So yes, artificial intelligence is actively shaping this vast framework, and its positive results are already evident.

Dr. Muhammad Shahzad:

How is artificial intelligence influencing our society, economy, and our fundamental worldviews?

Dr. Baland Iqbal:

That's an essential question. If AI is now addressing our basic needs—food, shelter, climate, education—then naturally, it will also affect our social structures, religious ideologies, and political and economic issues.

You may or may not agree with my perspective, but I believe that in terms of religious ideology or faith, there may not be much fundamental change, even amidst this technological revolution. Consider how religious institutions once rejected the radio and television but later embraced them as powerful tools for spreading their message. Today, religious bodies arguably have the strongest presence on print and electronic media—radio, microphones, computers, loudspeakers, and television.

The same pattern will likely repeat with AI and robotics. Initially dismissed, even mocked as attempts to "play God," these technologies will eventually be embraced. Religious institutions may begin extracting "prophecies" and "formulas" from sacred texts to justify these advancements. This dynamic isn't new—it's been present throughout history. The relationship between marketing, economic systems, and religion runs deep. AI will become deeply integrated with religious marketing and spiritual economies. Expect to see numerous apps loaded with religious content, widely used to promote spirituality.

Think about it—what once took place in mosques and temples before crowds of 40,000 to 50,000 people is now streamed to millions via YouTube and WhatsApp. Fundraising, donations, and other financial transactions tied to religious institutions are becoming easier through technology. Religion will increasingly use AI to its advantage.

Now, spirituality is a delicate matter, but worth mentioning. When it comes to politics, AI is already fully embedded. Five or six core components are reshaping political landscapes:

1. Social surveillance — Spy cameras track population behavior continuously.
2. Social censorship — AI tools are used to suppress or control information.
3. Social manipulation — This is rampant in societies like Pakistan.
4. Disinformation — Fake news and rumors deliberately confuse the public.
5. Internet control — Strategic use or shutdown of internet access to target populations.

Historically, during the Arab Spring, the internet played a key role in driving liberal change. But the same technology has since been used to enforce authoritarian control under the guise of democracy. It's all about using digital tools to steer citizens in specific directions.

A great book on this subject is *The Rise of Digital Repression: How Technology Is Reshaping Power, Politics, and Resistance* by Steven Feldstein. It explores how all forms of government—whether democratic, liberal, communist, or authoritarian—are being controlled through digital systems. The manipulation of populations has never been easier.

Coming back to spirituality, sectarianism, racism, even gender—their narratives are all evolving through digital technology. You'll find apps designed to transport users into metaphysical experiences using virtual headsets. With these, the physical world fades, replaced by a realm filled with celestial characters offering temporary spiritual comfort. Similarly, platforms for sexual satisfaction are emerging—websites and apps that use tokens to generate physical stimulation directly in erogenous zones. The rise of robotic wives and robotic girlfriends—customized by appearance, voice, and intellect to match individual fantasies—is no longer a futuristic dream. In many Western and Chinese markets, it's already a reality.

All of this indicates that we are developing an entirely new, AI-powered world—dramatically different from our traditional religious, social, sexual, and economic paradigms.

Dr. Muhammad Shahzad:

What sort of negative psychological impact is artificial intelligence having on us? In other words, what are we losing in return?

Dr. Baland Iqbal:

That's a very important question, Shahzad. We've spoken about many of the positive aspects of artificial intelligence—but we must also acknowledge the negative consequences.

To borrow Ghalib's sentiment:

"Don't ask about my state after you left—just look at yourself now that you're here."

I may not know how AI is doing behind my back, but I can definitely say that its presence has drastically altered my reality—for the worse.

We're seeing this most vividly in younger generations. They've become increasingly mechanical, preferring to live in the world of technology. Their emotional growth is stunted. Their ability to focus has diminished. We're witnessing issues with cognitive development. Stress, depression, and even suicide rates have risen alarmingly. Social interaction is nearly nonexistent. Loneliness is on the rise. Drug culture is more pervasive than ever.

Young people today have access to far more information than their emotional, intellectual, or experiential capacities can handle, leading to extreme mental pressure. The absence of genuine social contact is eroding trust. Suspicion and paranoia are increasing. Mental health issues have exploded.

Physically, we're also seeing more ailments—back pain, vision problems, joint diseases—largely from excessive screen use. And more broadly, we're facing social isolation, even economic loneliness, creating what I would call a full-blown social crisis.

In short: intelligence issues in children, memory problems, stunted social development, growing psychological disorders—these are all becoming more common among the youth. The damage is mounting, and for the sake of psychological and societal balance, we will eventually have to make some serious, collective decisions.

This mind must be restricted from thinking and speaking freely

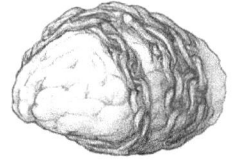

Dr. Muhammad Shahzad:

Doctor Iqbal, when we examine religious history in a general sense, do we come across different forms of blasphemy? In other words, does the term "blasphemy" appear repeatedly throughout history, albeit with evolving meanings? Can we say that blasphemy is not a new concept at all?

Dr. Baland Iqbal:

Look, Shahzad, if you study religious history objectively, you'll encounter a rather peculiar phenomenon. But before we get into that, let me point out that there's often a stark difference between religious history and anthropological-historical facts. Many events frequently referenced in divine scriptures or personalities described therein are not found in secular or non-religious historical records. The authenticity and historicity of such events are highly questionable. Yet, since these events have become part of sacred belief systems, their followers rarely seek to investigate their truth, nor do they show much interest.

For instance, in established historical records, we find no credible evidence or trace of figures like Adam, Eve, Abraham, or Moses, nor the 40-year sojourn through the wilderness of Canaan, nor the ancestral settlement of Jacob's people along the Nile, nor the well into which Joseph was cast by his brothers in Egypt. And yet, any random rock, crack, or landmark is accepted as sacred, and people are seen prostrating before it.

Now, if we look at the historical events in religious texts through this lens and consider the metaphorical implications of the term "blasphemy," we could argue that within the monotheistic traditions of the Middle East, the first "blasphemers" or dissenters from ancient religious traditions were prophets themselves. For example, Abraham himself rebelled against his father Azar's idols—those very deities that his father and tribe considered divine. Similarly, Moses defied the gods of Pharaoh, and Jesus was punished for similar defiance. Even Prophet Muhammad (PBUH) was considered a rebel and enemy by the Quraysh for his opposition to their ancestral beliefs.

From this perspective, the term *blasphemy* becomes largely meaningless. Regardless of its literal religious connotation, historically it has always referred to the rejection, denial, or rebellion against older traditions, gods, prophets, or scriptures. And such "blasphemous" acts are inevitably found at the roots of new religious or ideological movements. It is precisely this "denial" that has always been the catalyst for new thought and new consciousness—without which no intellectual revolution is possible.

The ironic part is that once these prophets or revolutionary leaders succeed, they too impose strict theological or constitutional doctrines, where any disagreement is again labeled "blasphemy." From Moses to the Prophet Muhammad (PBUH), we never find any permission granted to question their authority. Instead, the punishments for defiance are laid out in both this life and the hereafter.

This raises the question: Why do these prophets, who were themselves revolutionaries in their own time, attempt to suppress opposition after their mission? The answer is that they realize the survival of their own ideology depends on rigid preservation—enforced through strength and strict boundaries. Otherwise, just as they once challenged the old, someone will eventually challenge them too.

In short, if we approach religious history not through blind faith but with the lens of a historian or anthropologist, we'll see that whether it's a secular authoritarian state or a religious one, challenging foundational ideologies—whether political or theological—brings equally harsh consequences. The only difference is that in the religious context, these punishments are sanctified, redefined as sins or blasphemies, and thereby placed beyond the reach of reason or justice. Judgment becomes a matter of blind faith rather than evidence or debate.

The even more painful reality is that in such cases, the right to punish often falls into the hands of anyone and everyone, resulting in widespread social anarchy, and society begins to resemble the tribal age—because such thinking is inherently tribal.

Dr. Muhammad Shahzad:

If we separate freedom of thought and expression from religion and examine it in the secular world, we still find similar examples. For instance, in Greece, five centuries before the birth of Jesus, the foundations of democracy were being laid, yet Socrates was forced to drink poison simply for expressing his views. How would you compare these two spheres?

Dr. Baland Iqbal:

It's all about tradition. History repeatedly shows that whether religious or secular, whenever certain traditions are deemed politically useful by authoritarian regimes, those regimes go to any lengths—political, social, economic, religious, or otherwise—to preserve them.

This was explained eloquently by Italian philosopher and political theorist Niccolò Machiavelli in the 16th century in his book *The Prince*, where he wrote that "any immoral tactic used to achieve political gain is a form of political ethics."

So, when political benefits begin to flow from religious ideologies, political and religious powers shake hands behind closed doors to strengthen each other. You can observe this clearly throughout Islamic religious history—from the Umayyads to the fall of Baghdad, from the Ottoman Empire to the Mughal period. Political and religious interests constantly intertwine.

After the 15th century, as the West entered an age of social, political, scientific, and philosophical enlightenment, we notice an odd contrast in the East. In the East, religion was heavily employed in service of colonialism. This *selective evolution of difference* becomes clearly visible in how religion was used to manipulate Eastern societies for political ends. Thus, we see a *selective renaissance*—a controlled and filtered version of enlightenment.

As a result, Eastern societies, especially intellectually, began to decay even more. Authors like Edward Said and Noam Chomsky have discussed these issues in depth. This is why we find in history that struggles for freedom of expression in the East have had to fight a *dual battle*—against both religious and secular authoritarianism—whereas in the West, the struggle was mostly against secular or non-religious authoritarianism.

Dr. Muhammad Shahzad:

Doctor Iqbal, issues surrounding freedom of expression are not limited to politics or religion. The society we live in has its own evolutionary background. Many abnormal customs have unfortunately become normalized values, which are "respected" and protected. What is your opinion on this?

Dr. Baland Iqbal:

Indeed, we face two major collisions. First, there are the ancient traditions and so-called values of our own society that we insist on preserving—values that are not visible in Western civilizational contexts. As we integrate into a global world, these values often clash in significant ways.

For example, ours is a patriarchal society. Patriarchal values have almost become part of our DNA. However, we see similar values even in Western societies—for instance, the phenomenon of *white privilege*, despite their global outlook. Similarly, we face issues of minority rights, whether it's the treatment of gay, lesbian, or transgender individuals in India or Pakistan. We cannot simply ignore these realities.

Then there are women's rights, child labor, and sexual abuse—issues that have become deeply ingrained in societal structures. If such so-called customs or values—religious or secular—have, over centuries, become normalized social norms, then we must rigorously analyze and critique them.

In my view, the direct responsibility for catalyzing change in social thought and consciousness lies with intellectuals—those organically embedded in society. Whether poets, writers, psychologists, philosophers, artists, dramatists, or media professionals—they carry an ethical duty to continuously challenge political, religious, or social opposition and offer the public a revolutionary intellectual awareness.

I believe, Shahzad, that you and I are among these organic thinkers—engaged in an unending effort to examine and articulate these themes. We are not just discussing them but also working to shape them into books—so that, in our own modest way, we can light a lamp of awareness and provide some guidance for the next generation.

The Last Question

Dr. Muhammad Shahzad:

One last question — completely different from the rest of this book's themes. It's a question that lives in the heart of every young person, and everyone has their own interpretation of it. What is your take on love? Have you ever experienced it? What exactly is this emotion?

Dr. Baland Iqbal:

Shahzad, I believe this is the most difficult question in the entire book. If the human being is the greatest mystery in the universe, then love is the deepest, most mysterious emotion — one that cannot be fully explained by psychology, philosophy, or even literature.

Yes, I have experienced it. And honestly, what kind of human hasn't? But love is such a deeply personal feeling that it often needs no words for expression. It lives in silences, glances, gestures.

In my view, when love enters a person, they cease to be just a biological being and are transformed into an emotional one — from matter into pure feeling. When I experienced this emotion, I felt a strange transformation within myself. As a man, my heart longed for only one thing: to escape the tragic fate of the men described in Oscar Wilde's haunting poem The Ballad of Reading Gaol — and instead, to love like a woman. Because when a woman loves, she only loves — with her entire being, without hesitation, without ego, and without calculation. Let me share with you that unforgettable poem, which so deeply shaped this realization:

The Ballad of Reading Gaol by Oscar Wilde

Yet each man kills the thing he loves
By each let this be heard,
Some do it with a bitter look,
Some with a flattering word,
The coward does it with a kiss,
The brave man with a sword!

Some kill their love when they are young,
And some when they are old;
Some strangle with the hands of Lust,
Some with the hands of Gold:
The kindest use a knife, because
The dead so soon grow cold.

Some love too little, some too long,
Some sell, and others buy;
Some do the deed with many tears,
And some without a sigh:
For each man kills the thing he loves,
Yet each man does not die.

This poem reveals the tragic truth: men often destroy the very thing they claim to love. And I, too, feared becoming one of them. That is why I wished to love not with possession or pride, but with surrender — like a woman who becomes only love.

www.ingramcontent.com/pod-product-compliance
Lightning Source LLC
Chambersburg PA
CBHW052030030426
42337CB00027B/4932